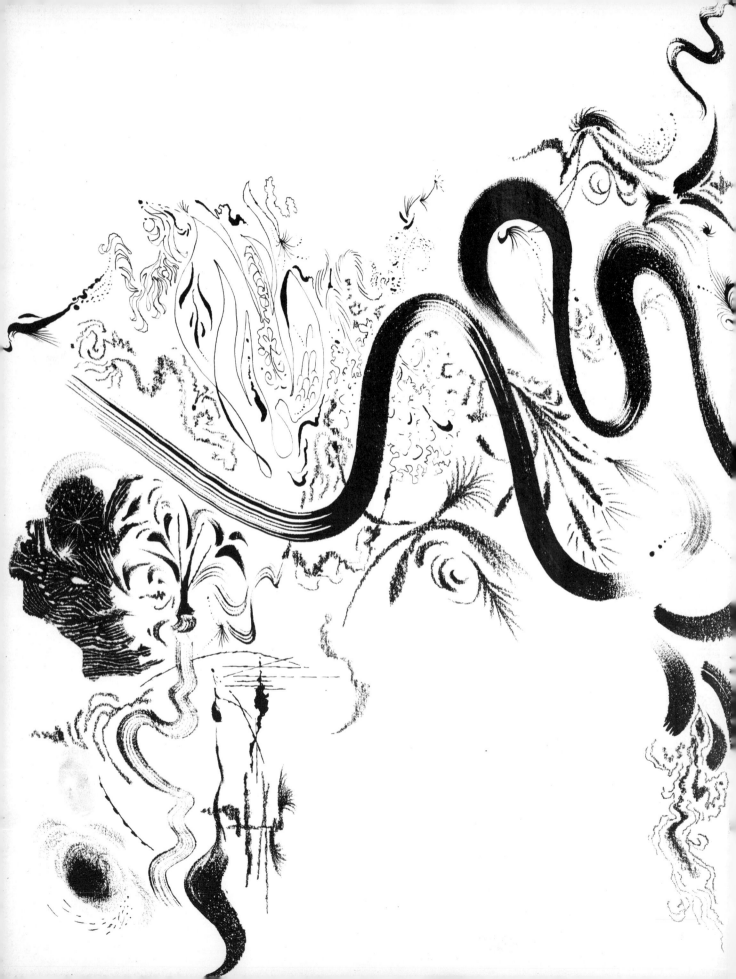

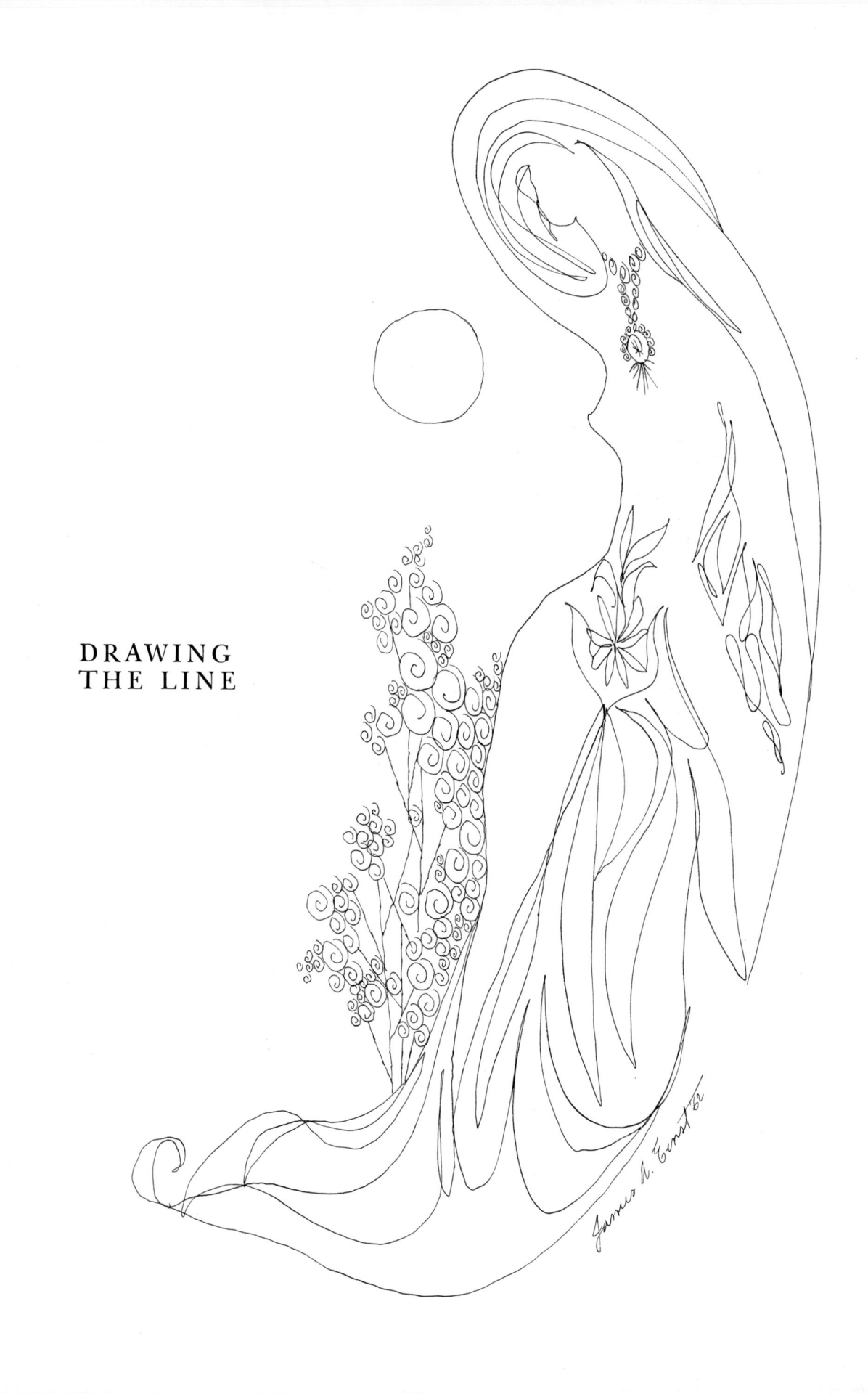

DRAWING
THE LINE

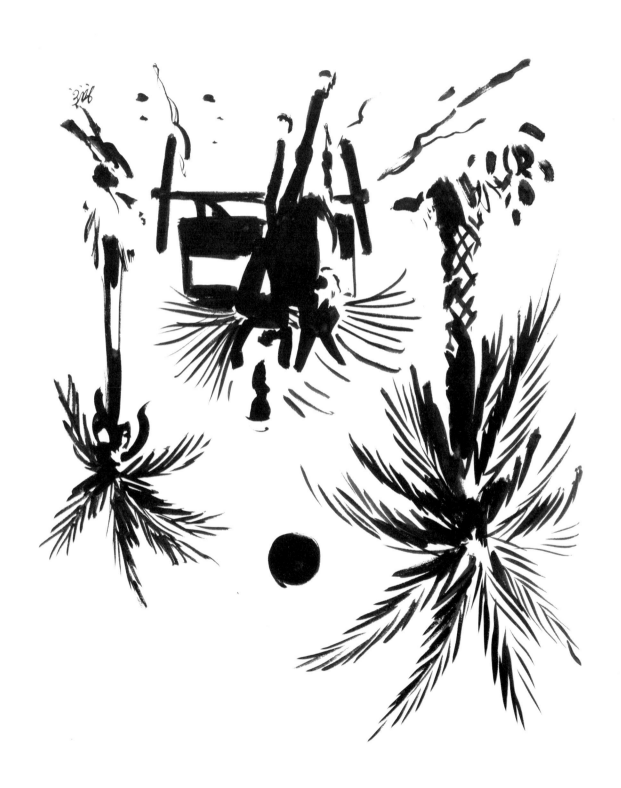

DRAWING
THE LINE

FINE AND COMMERCIAL ART

JAMES A. ERNST

REINHOLD PUBLISHING
CORPORATION · NEW YORK

© 1962, Reinhold Publishing Corporation
All rights reserved
Printed in the United States of America
Library of Congress catalog card no. 62-10719
Designed by James A. Ernst
Printed by The Comet Press, Inc.
Bound by Van Rees Book Binding Corporation
Second Printing, 1965

to a. e.

without whom . . . .

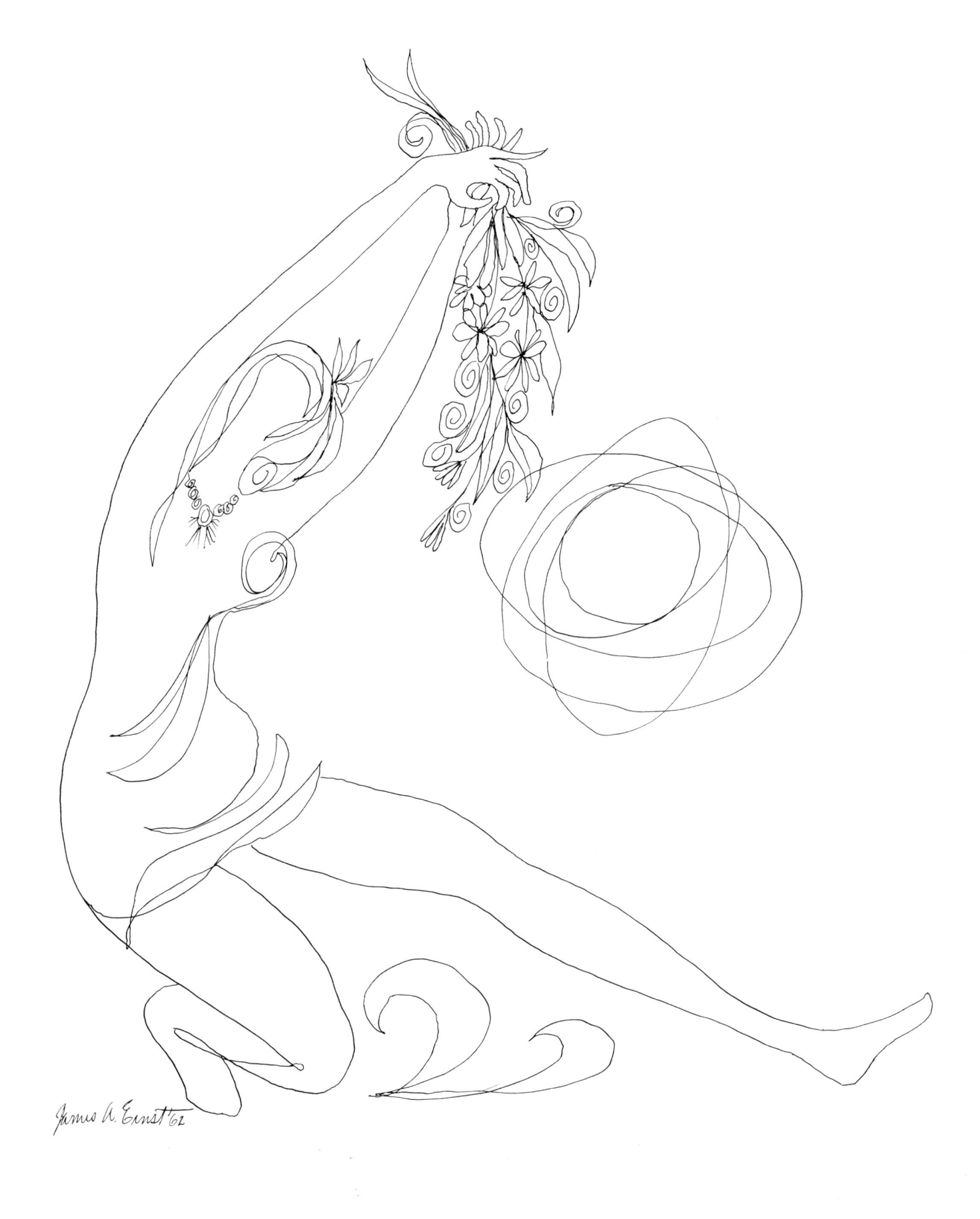

James A. Ernst '62

CONTENTS

FOREWORD by Harold W. Olsen   9

WHY DRAW THE LINE?   11

DESIGN IN LINE   15

THE PIVOT METHOD   23

PEN AND INK   25
    The Decorative Continuous Line   31
    The Broken Line   39
    Continuous and Broken Lines   43
    The Textured Line   51
    The Thick and Thin Line   55
    Combined Pen Lines   59

SPECIAL DRAWING PENS   69

BRUSH WITH INK OR PAINT   77
    The Crisp Line   81
    The Dry Brush Line   83
    The Split Brush Line   87
    The Broken Line   89

PEN AND BRUSH COMBINED   93

ERRORS AND CORRECTIONS   99

PENCILS, STICKS, AND CRAYONS   103
    The Lead Pencil Line   105
    The Carbon Pencil Line   109
    The Lithographic, Grease, or Wax Pencil Line   111
    The Charcoal Line   115
    The Pastel Line   121

SCRATCHBOARD   127

THE LINE IN COMMERCIAL ART   137

END OF THE LINE   155

Frontispiece. Line drawing with brush and paint on bond paper.

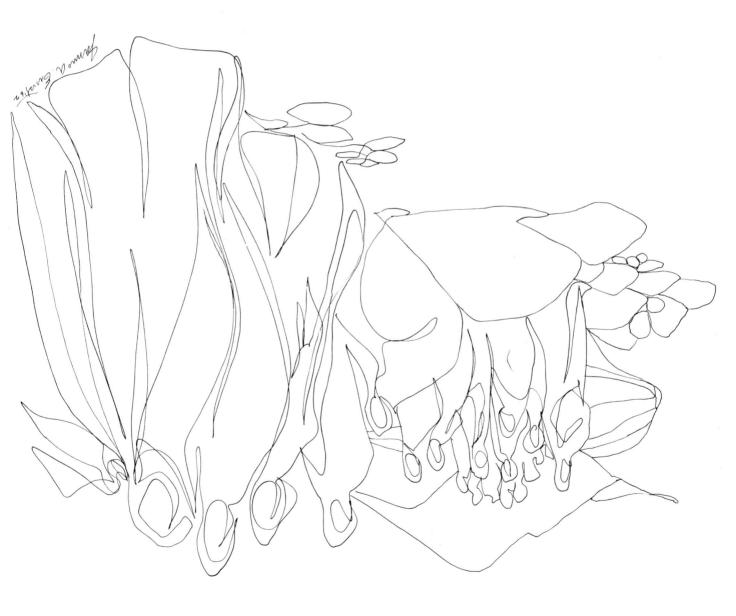

FOREWORD

Is line drawing still an important technique in the graphic arts?

For centuries, line drawing was man's major means of communication. It was generally realistic in style. After the introduction of new techniques of reproduction which could render realism easier, faster, and better than line, the style of line drawing varied from the realistic to a more interpretive handling.

Radio, television, and motion pictures have also affected printed media techniques because of the increased exposure of the public to mass communication. Today, billions of dollars are spent each year in reaching the public. The rate of boredom, due to this exposure, has increased. What used to remain fresh and distinctive for years, now loses its effectiveness in months. As a result, industry has placed a premium on imaginative visual change of pace in order to be seen and noticed in this competitive situation. Every technique is explored by graphic designers, in all media, in pursuit of the public's attention.

Many of our major magazines have revised their formats to make use of the faster, simpler, and stronger design approaches that add visual excitement to their presentation of ideas. Linear design has provided a strong area for impact in the change of pace from photography, and illustrators are making effective use of it.

To answer the question above, then, line drawing is not any less effective or less important today than in the past. It is still a major technique of the graphic designer, but the style of handling has changed over the years, as it will continue to change in the future. Its only limitation will be the creative talent and imagination of the artists using it. In the hands of the right artist, line drawing can still provide distinctive, fresh, exciting visual presentation of ideas.

HAROLD W. OLSEN
Vice President in charge of Art
Batten, Barton, Durstine & Osborn, Inc.

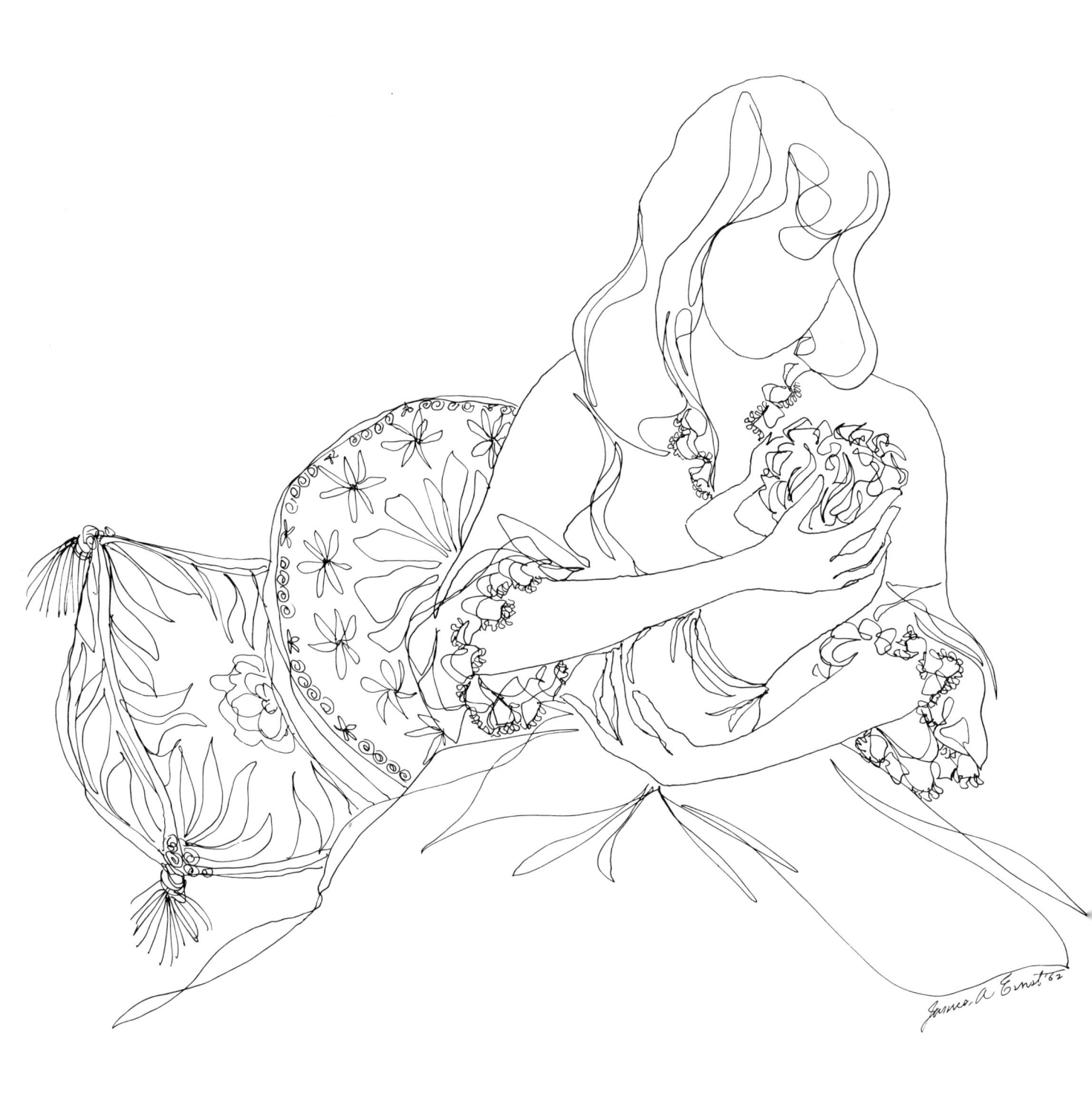

WHY DRAW THE LINE?

There are times when ideas seem to work out only when I have a pen in my hand. I need the rhythm and grace and flow of the fine pen line to express what I want to set down. Or sometimes it is a bold black brush stroke which must outline the picture that is in my mind. Though I enjoy working over a canvas with oils, or may be at my best with water colors, there are times when only the line will do for me.

The line of black on white, unfused with tone and color, can be crisp or vague, sharp or blunt, sweeping or meticulous. It can simulate tone without use of tone. It is of infinite variety, for each type of line—whether it is the heavy line, the textured line, the thick-and-thin line—takes on still another character from the hand of its user. Matisse's line, for instance, is totally unlike Ben Shahn's. George Price uses a different line from Steig, and Steig from Soglow.

Perhaps because I do a great deal of drawing, I have experimented with a number of different kinds of lines. Since pen and ink are my preference, most of my line variations come from changes in stroke, keeping the same tools. Many more variations can be worked out, however, by changing tools (pencil, brush, felt-tip, knife), or fluid (India ink, black paint), or paper (textured, stippled, scratchboard). Examples of such variations are set forth in this book.

Whatever the equipment used, there is one inescapable prerequisite—practice, always more practice. The line is a ruthless taskmaster: each stroke must be right the first time, for patching or correcting is likely either to be obvious and therefore ineffective, or to take so much time and trouble that it would have been simpler to have started over after the first slip.

Only in commercial work, where photographic reproduction is to follow, can pasted patches and white paint save the day. Even so, such remedies had better be reserved for those times

when the work is right but the client wants "just a slight change." To compete in the commercial field, an artist must be able to do work of high calibre with a promptness that allows no time for scratches and patches. The skill for facile drawing can be developed through consistent practice.

A cardinal rule for the line man was offered long ago by a Roman artist, Apelles, whose art seems to have disappeared though his wisdom has been preserved. In the words of a historian, "It was a custom with Apelles, to which he most tenaciously adhered, never to let any day pass, however busy he might be, without exercising himself by drawing some outline or other." From this good habit came a primary rule for the aspiring line man, "No day without a line!"

The same sage gave us another proverb, upon which, I think it is safe to say, all artists set their warm and vigorous approval. When Apelles completed a painting, he followed a practice of

putting it on the street in front of his studio and then hiding where he could listen for the reactions of passersby. When a shoemaker paused to criticize one of his works because a shoe in the picture had "more latchets on one side than the other," the artist spoke out with his opinion of shoemakers as art critics, and gave us the handy proverb, "Let the cobbler stick to his last!"

In commercial work, there is wide opportunity for the use of line. Some problems can be resolved only with this technique; for other situations, it may be the best of several methods. For an advertisement surrounded by columns of print, for instance, a line drawing can be more arresting than a halftone. There is the additional important commercial advantage that line lends itself to good reproduction at low cost.

For the fine artist, the factor of reproduction has little or no bearing. His concern is with the expression of his idea in the original work, and, as I have said (and will try to avoid repeating

too often), there are times when only the line will do—when the delicacy or the drama or the quality of simple statement can be executed best in line.

I know of no rules to lay down governing when to choose this medium. As much as anything, it is a matter of how an individual responds to it. This is a little like Lincoln's comment when an author pressed him for a testimonial on a new book. The reluctant Lincoln wrote, in essence: For those who like this kind of book, this is just the kind of book they would like.

For those, then, who like the line—who recognize its flexibility, its variety, its directness, who enjoy the feel of the pen, the pencil, the stick, or whatever—for them, line drawing will best express some of the things they have to say. This book attempts to contribute to the success and satisfaction of "getting into line."

DESIGN IN LINE

To draw a line and to make it achieve what you want it to achieve requires skill—to handle pen and ink without catastrophe, to control weight of line and direction. Yet, no matter how skillfully lines may be executed, a drawing must have good design to be successful.

Such a conclusion may seem too obvious to deserve mention, yet design is so fundamental to line drawing that it cannot be emphasized too much. Here there is no combination of colors to cloak inadequate composition, no fusing of tones to obscure poor design. A drawing is strong or weak, according to its structure.

I think of the fundamental elements of design in line as size and shape, value, texture, motion, and rhythm.

The *size and shape* of the forms which compose a drawing are conditioned primarily by the idea to be expressed. For instance,

dimension

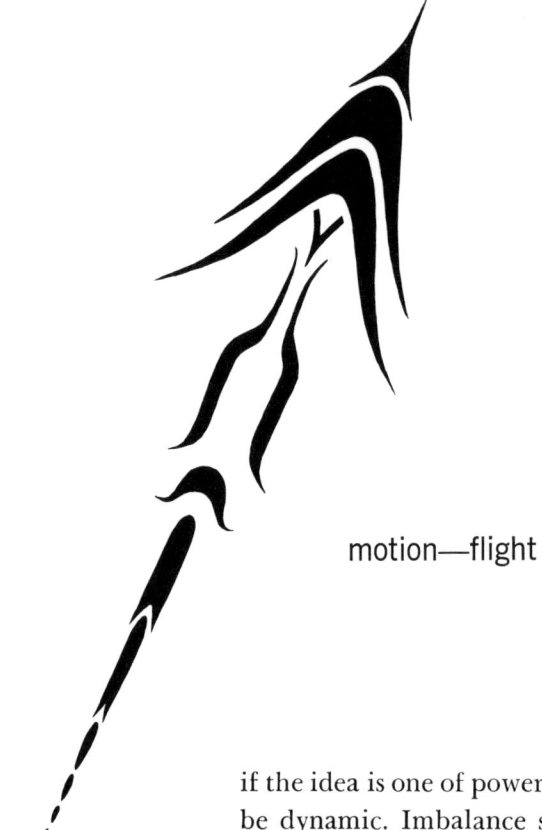

motion—flight

if the idea is one of power and excitement, sizes and shapes should be dynamic. Imbalance should be created through unequal relationships of the sizes and shapes of forms and their dissimilar directions.

On the other hand, if peace and calm are the mood, equal sizes with similar shapes and directions work toward the effect desired. The result should be one of harmony and balance.

Space relationships give dimension to a drawing. Overlapping forms, for instance, tend to create an illusion of depth, as do forms of similar shape placed next to each other with successive decrease in size and in distance apart. (Visualize a row of trees receding down a lane, for instance.) Depth can also be achieved in the use of a single line which flows from thick to thin.

The two-dimensional extension of space—the breadth and height of the picture field—also results from the relative position of forms. Lines, dots, or solids placed close together contract an area; if they are spread apart, continuing to the edge of the field, they suggest an expansion of the boundaries.

DESIGN

IN

LINE

16

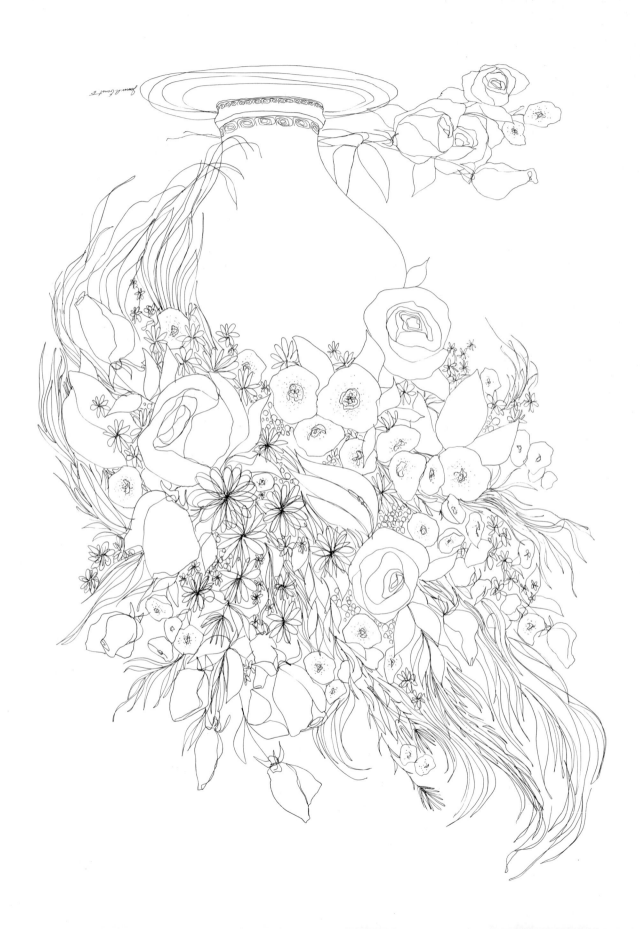

For the break-up of areas to give pleasing spatial relation, which is only another way of referring to good design, there is no clearer example, to my mind, than the work of Mondrian.

Value also can be used to achieve a third dimension. By the use of modeling, lines or dots or a combination of both concentrated and gradually dispersed within a shape, form can be obtained. Usually the white of the paper provides the lightest value, with solid black the darkest. The intermediate values come from the weight of lines used, or the closeness of one line to another. The contrast in value—that is, in degree of darkness—of one form to another again influences the feeling of space. If, for instance, one draws three heavy lines, unequal in size and in distance from each other, and two light lines, also dissimilar

in size and distance, the dark lines come forward in space and the light ones tend to recede.

Texture lends interest to drawing. It gives a change of pace which avoids monotony. The almost infinite range of textures, which can be achieved with different kinds of lines or dots, is suggested by the techniques illustrated in the following chapters of this book.

Motion adds greatly to the general mood in the expression of an idea. It is closely allied with space and direction. As an example, a short line drawn at an angle near the top of the picture field can create an illusion of motion. By adding direction through the thickening of the line at its base, the motion of falling is suggested. If the greatest width of the line is at the top, the

illusion is of thrust or ascent. A staggering of such lines behind the first, aimed in the same direction either upward or downward, gives the illusion of increasing motion.

Rhythm unites the elements of a drawing, giving it grace and flow through continuity of line whether drawn or implied. A series of such rhythmic motions, repeated in the picture, heightens the mood and enhances the idea to be expressed.

The integration of *rhythm* and *motion* in a drawing, the development of *texture*, the manipulation of *values* and spatial relations, all dealt with only as factors, won't necessarily result in good design any more than including pointed arches, a rose window, and towers in a structure creates a Gothic cathedral. Basic knowledge, skill, and taste are the essentials which combine elements into a satisfying whole, or, in this instance, give good design to a line drawing.

DESIGN IN LINE

Simple shapes • dark against light, light against dark.

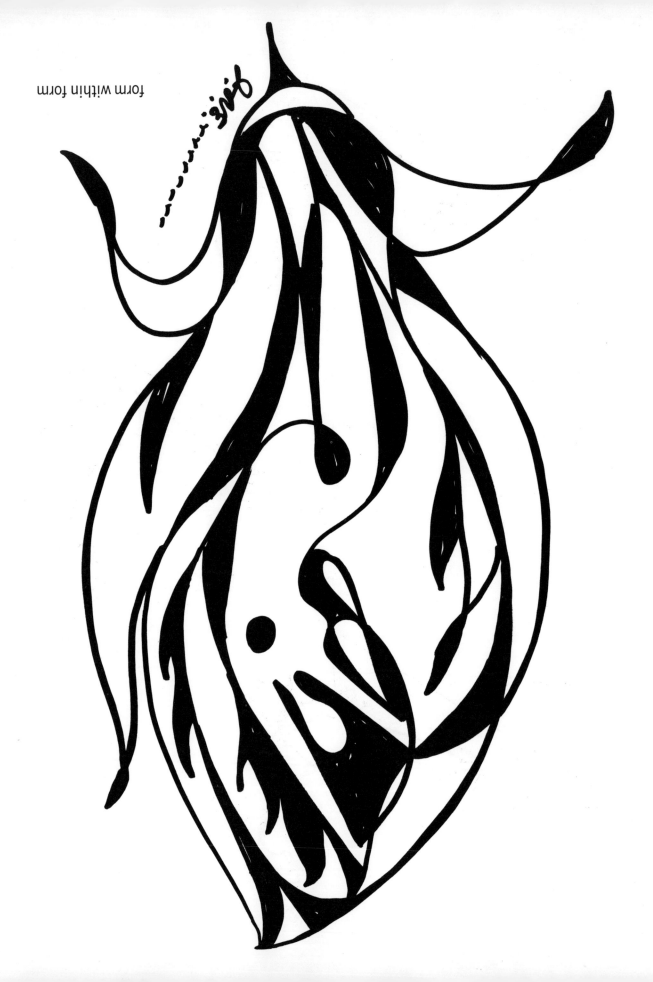

form within form

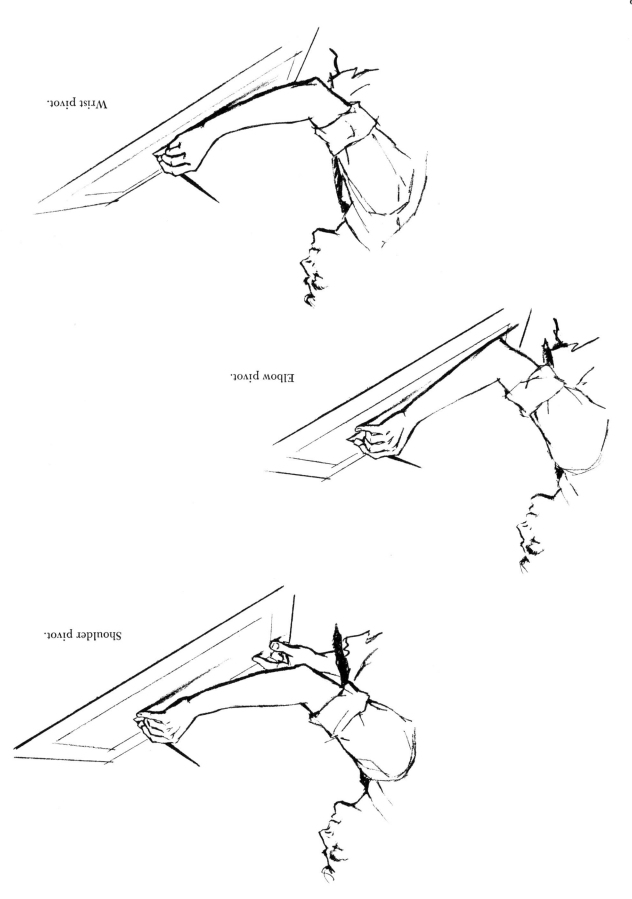

Wrist pivot.

Elbow pivot.

Shoulder pivot.

THE PIVOT METHOD

One day I discovered that, over the years, I had unconsciously evolved three ways of drawing. For close, detailed work, I rest my arm on the board, with wrist fairly firm, and work with the fingers, as one may do in writing. For the freest motion, for an unimpeded sweep over the paper, my hand and arm swing loosely from the shoulder. In between, like most compromises, comes a combination of the two. Pivoting from the elbow allows some freedom of movement with considerable control of detail.

This pivot method can function for any type of line drawn with a motion from any one of the pivot points: the shoulder, the elbow, or the wrist.

The shoulder pivot invites the maximum freedom of line. I tilt my working tool some twenty-five degrees off the vertical and swing my stroke from the shoulder, with nothing but the little finger touching the paper, extended as a control point for the evenness and weight of line.

With the elbow pivot, again the little finger is extended to the working surface, the tool tilted further away from the vertical to perhaps forty-five degrees.

The wrist pivot obviously has no need for the finger control since the whole side of the hand rests on the board to give complete support and maximum control for working.

Best results with the shoulder pivot come with direct drawing. The vaguest kind of sketch may designate general areas, but it would defeat the purpose to try to ink in a preliminary drawing using the shoulder pivot. With the elbow pivot, a rough sketch may well be followed, rather than working directly.

An experiment with the pivot method can be more convincing than an explanation. Draw a simple design, some circles, or a series of lines. The briefest sketch will demonstrate the effect and the experience. Change the tools from pen to brush to pencil, and so on. The variations and the advantages will be apparent.

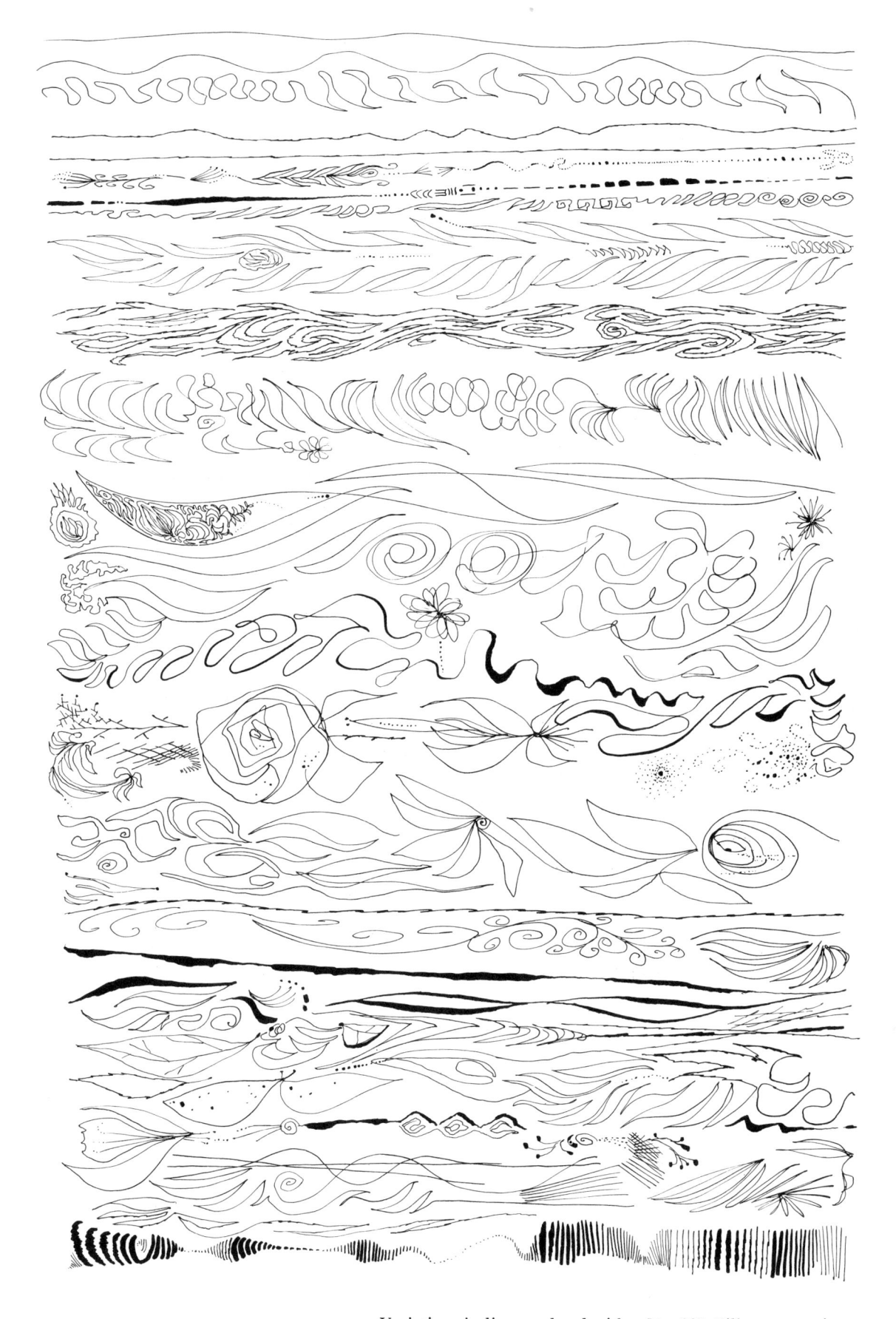

Variations in line rendered with a No. 290 Gillott pen point.

PEN AND INK

Almost any artist will admit to catalogue perusing as his "favorite indoor sport." Leafing through pages of the art dealer's wares can beguile one from work and consume enough time to have finished the job on one's conscience. Coming upon a favorite manufacturer is like meeting an old friend and finding out what he is doing now. A familiar pen number crops up, new papers are suggested, and time gets away.

For pen and ink work, experience has brought me a wide range of acquaintances but a restricted number of old friends who serve me well. In inks there are two which have best met my demands. They are Higgins India Ink and Pelikan Opaque Black. There are many others, of course; the choice developing as a matter of personal experience and preference.

All inks have a tendency to congeal slightly from exposure to air when the bottle top has been removed. As an artist who knows the difficulty this can cause, let me offer some suggestions.

Don't shake the ink bottle! For finished work, I find it best to use a new bottle, or at least one that has not been left uncorked for any considerable time. As a matter of fact, I always keep the ink bottle corked, except when I am filling my pen—and I do mean filling, not dipping. I use the quill in the bottle top to pour or lay the ink on my pen point. This not only moves me to set the cork back on the bottle; it saves me from smearing the ink from the mouth of the bottle on my penholder and subsequently on my fingers. Obviously one is careful when handling India ink, but I make certain to keep a white blotter handy anyway.

As to penholders, the artist must select those which feel most comfortable in his grip, and there are many varieties to choose from. Some holders have grips of cork, others rubber, wood, or metal, and some are grooved or spiraled. My preference is for

a large cork grip, probably because I have a large hand and can hold such a pen more easily. Besides, I like the feel of cork.

Pen points are of many kinds, the manufacturers' products I know best being Gillott, Esterbrook, Hunt, and Brandauer. Each presents a wide range of points, but the ones which have tested the most satisfactorily for my purposes are Esterbrook—Nos. 356, 355, 354, 358, 357, and crow quill 62; Gillott—290, 291, 170, 303, 404, and crow quill 659; Hunt—99, 100, 103, 22, 56, and crow quill 102; Brandauer—0131, 517, 515, 303, and crow quill 311. These represent variations chiefly in fineness and flexibility. The crow quills are good for extremely fine line work. Their points are very flexible. There are two points that I use most often and which will do just about everything for me. The 290 Gillott is very fine and exceptionally flexible; Gillott 170 gives me a slightly heavier line and is much firmer.

The care and cleaning of pen points is a serious matter for the serious artist. This is not because the cost of pen points is excessive: it isn't the money, it's the principle, and the principle in this case is a selfish one. It takes time to break in a new point. Once broken in, it works much more easily, and thus one postpones shifting to a new one as long as possible.

Best results come from cleaning the pen point frequently while working, in order to maintain a free flow of ink. Regular cleaners or chamois pen wipers are good; my preference is to wipe the point with a piece of tracing paper. If the ink does dry on the point and begins to give a gritty feel, it can be scraped off with a single-edge razor blade or a sharp knife. If water is used to clean the point, one must be certain the point is dry before reapplying ink. Unless this precaution is taken, the ink will become somewhat diluted and produce a greyish, off-black line.

When points are not in use, I have found it advisable to keep

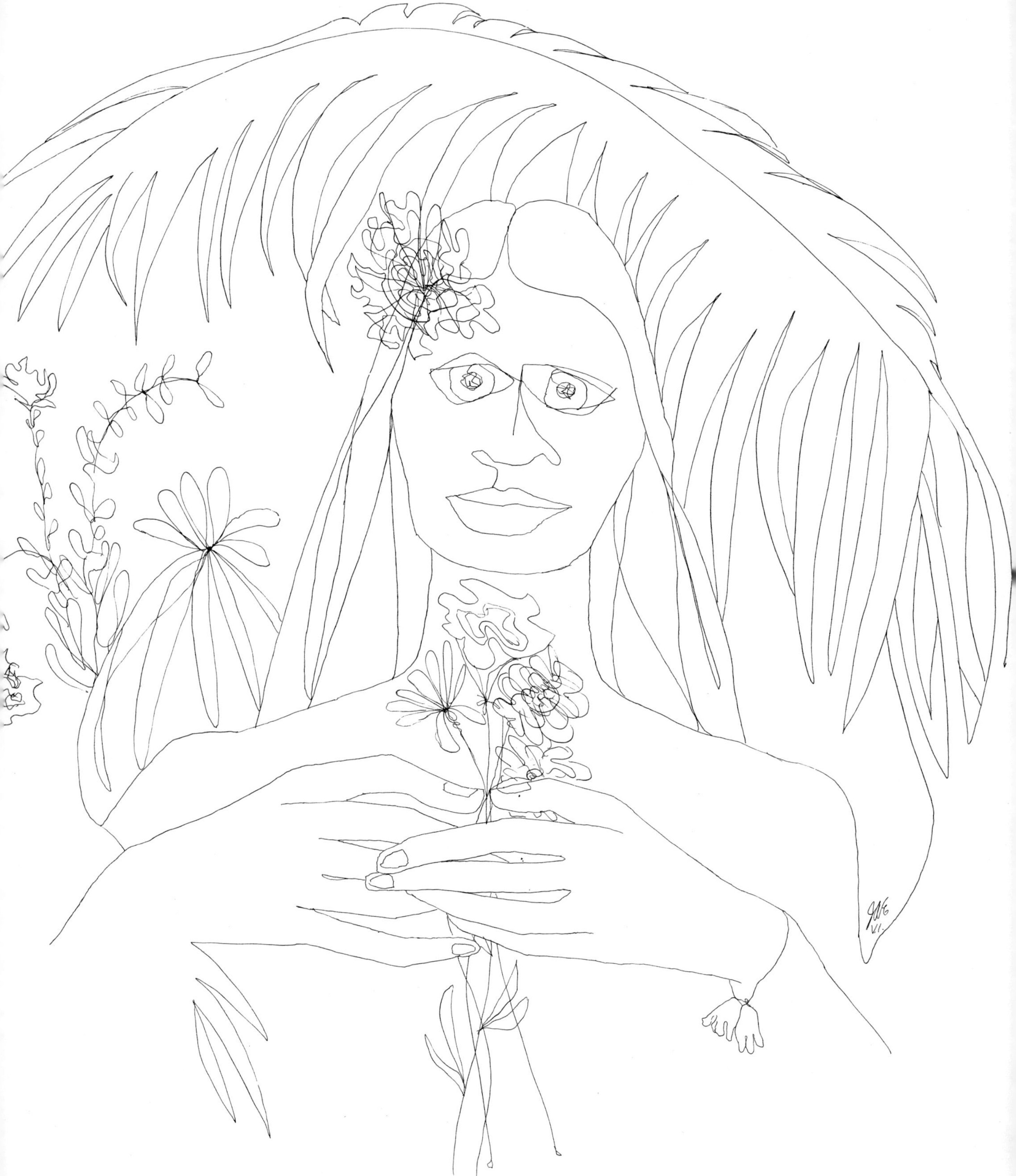

them in a small container, away from other tools to avoid damage to the points.

Ultimately, wear and tear or lack of care will enforce the retirement of a point and a new one must be initiated. To dispel the slightly oily protective film, apply to the point a little of the fluid agent called "non-crawl"—or a little of the fluid agent called saliva; add a drop or two of ink and then let it set. After a few minutes, make test markings on a piece of paper, and the new point should be ready for work.

Varieties of drawing papers and boards are numerous. With extremely glossy surfaces, the pen line has a tendency to spread or run and become a little wider. If the surface is too rough, the pen may catch, causing splatter on the paper and difficulty for the artist. I like the fairly smooth surfaces without gloss, such as kid-finish Strathmore; cold pressed Whatman paper, medium surface; ledger pad and bond pad paper. Through trial and error, each artist will arrive at the working surfaces which suit him best.

The angle of the drawing board is important. I prefer a tilt of about twenty-five to thirty degrees from the horizontal, which seems to be pretty generally what I see many others use, though there are also variations from the nearly flat to the fairly steep. Once an artist finds the most comfortable slant for him, he is likely to stay with it for much of his work, changing only when he moves to a radically different kind of piece.

The board angle may remain fairly constant, but the position of the pa-

per on the board does not. It is turned as the artist works, seeking to achieve a better stroke for a line. As a left-hander, I may shift my paper more often than most do—in fact, I shift it almost continuously as I work, partly to keep my arm from smearing what I have already drawn.

The technical subject of proper lighting is not one that I am qualified to deal with; but I can speak with a voice of experience in emphasizing one precaution. Be sure to avoid glare from the working surface. Glare will interfere with the quality of your work, and so will the headache and eyestrain which it causes.

Another important physical factor in the quality of work is a steady hand. I have noticed that on some days my hand is less steady than usual and fine line work becomes hazardous. On such occasions, and also at the times when I get finger cramps from holding the pen, I use an exercise borrowed from boxing, though with a variation. I clench my fist tightly, then extend the fingers hard—close, then open, briskly and firmly—for a minute or two, as if with the boxer's rubber ball. (Those who have contributed their pints to the Red Cross will recognize in this, also, the instructions of the supervising nurse.)

Occasionally, while working, I stop, let my arm hang loosely from the shoulder, and shake it for a couple of minutes. Both these exercises seem to help me, and soon I am ready to work again, much relaxed.

I have mentioned finger cramps from holding the pen. They usually come from gripping it too tightly, a tendency which heightens as tension builds during a long job and the muscles unconsciously grow more rigid. A light, easy hold on the pen makes for better drawing.

It is a good idea to stop for a few minutes out of every hour and go through some such relaxing motions as I have suggested, for greater comfort in continued work. In fact, I think comfort —or more exactly the absence of discomfort—has considerable bearing on art accomplishment. A good angle of board for eyes and arm, a paper to which one adapts readily, a comfortable pen grip, a responsive point, all contribute to satisfying work.

the

decorative

continuous

line

The free-flowing line is perhaps the most difficult to execute successfully, yet to me it is the most satisfying line in the graphic field. For such work, there should be very little—preferably no—preliminary drawing to hamper the stroke. Freedom and spontaneity should be the characteristics; a sketch-guided line is likely to appear belabored and stilted.

If a light pencil drawing must be made in advance, it should serve only as a suggestion, with no effort on the part of the artist to follow it exactly. It is better to make a fairly complete pencil drawing on another sheet of paper for the purpose of fixing the picture in one's mind. Once this is done and studied, the artist should be better able to translate the picture freely to his final sheet.

Most often I find myself using the Gillott 290 pen point. It allows me maximum freedom, offers the greatest flexibility, and produces a very delicate line.

I usually prefer an even weight for this kind of work, in which case the pressure applied to the pen point must remain meticulously constant. Yet I do vary the weight occasionally in several ways. One is by pressure; bearing down more heavily swings a

PEN

AND

INK

Decorative continuous line drawing on ledger pad paper, Gillott 290 pen. Note the freedom of movement with this line.

thin line into a broader stroke. Again, when changing the direction of a line without turning the pen—as in, for instance, drawing a vertical line with the flat of the point, leading into a horizontal one moving sideways—the weight can change from wide stroke to hairline thin. Holding the pen at a flatter or steeper angle to the paper will also change the line.

My alternate preference to the 290 is the Gillott 170 pen point. This produces a slightly heavier weight line. It is not nearly as flexible and perhaps for this reason may be more easily controlled.

To refer to the pivot method, it is the shoulder pivot stroke that achieves the greatest freedom for the decorative continuous line. Using this stroke of necessity moves the artist farther away from the working plane, encouraging a looser motion. I hold the pen at an angle of about twenty-five degrees from the vertical and rest the extended little finger on the paper as a control. It is the rigidity of the finger which aids in maintaining a line of even weight.

My next point may seem either negligible or significant to the reader, depending upon his own experience in drawing. In mine, I have found breath control important to a free-flowing line. If possible, the artist should hold his breath while making a line of any sweep. By doing so, he produces an uninterrupted line, whereas taking a breath in mid-stroke has a tendency to alter it, the degree of deviation of course differing among individuals. Holding the breath can avoid what might otherwise look like a slight hesitation in the work, suggesting unsureness on the part of the artist. The sureness of the stroke and its freedom are essential to the decorative continuous line.

PEN
AND
INK

33

Decorative continuous line drawing on
bond pad paper, Gillott 290 pen.

Decorative continuous line drawing on bond pad paper, Esterbrook pen No. 355. This pen compares with the Gillott 290.

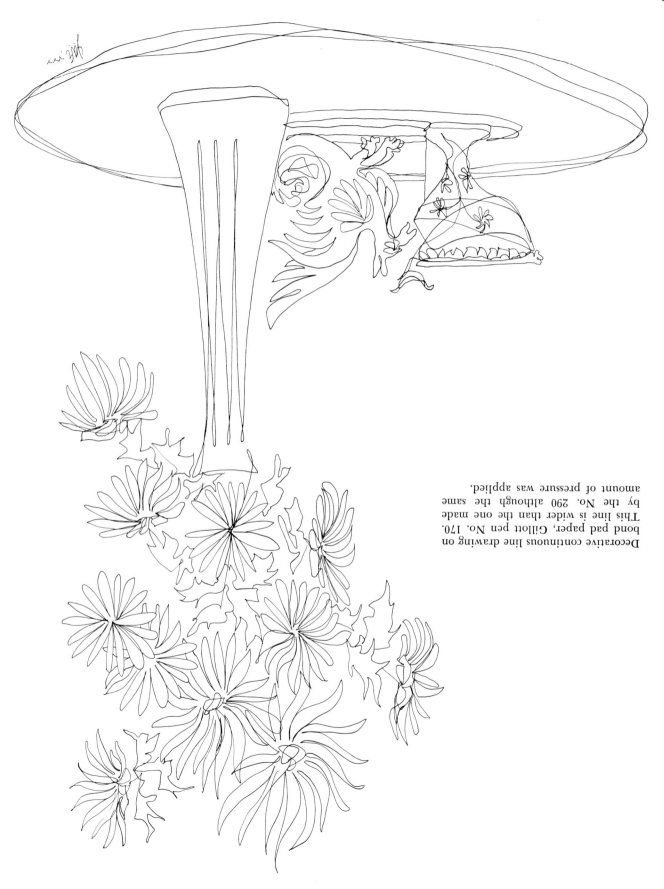

Decorative continuous line drawing on bond pad paper, Gillott pen No. 170. This line is wider than the one made by the No. 290 although the same amount of pressure was applied.

Decorative continuous line drawing on
bond pad paper, Gillott pen No. 170.

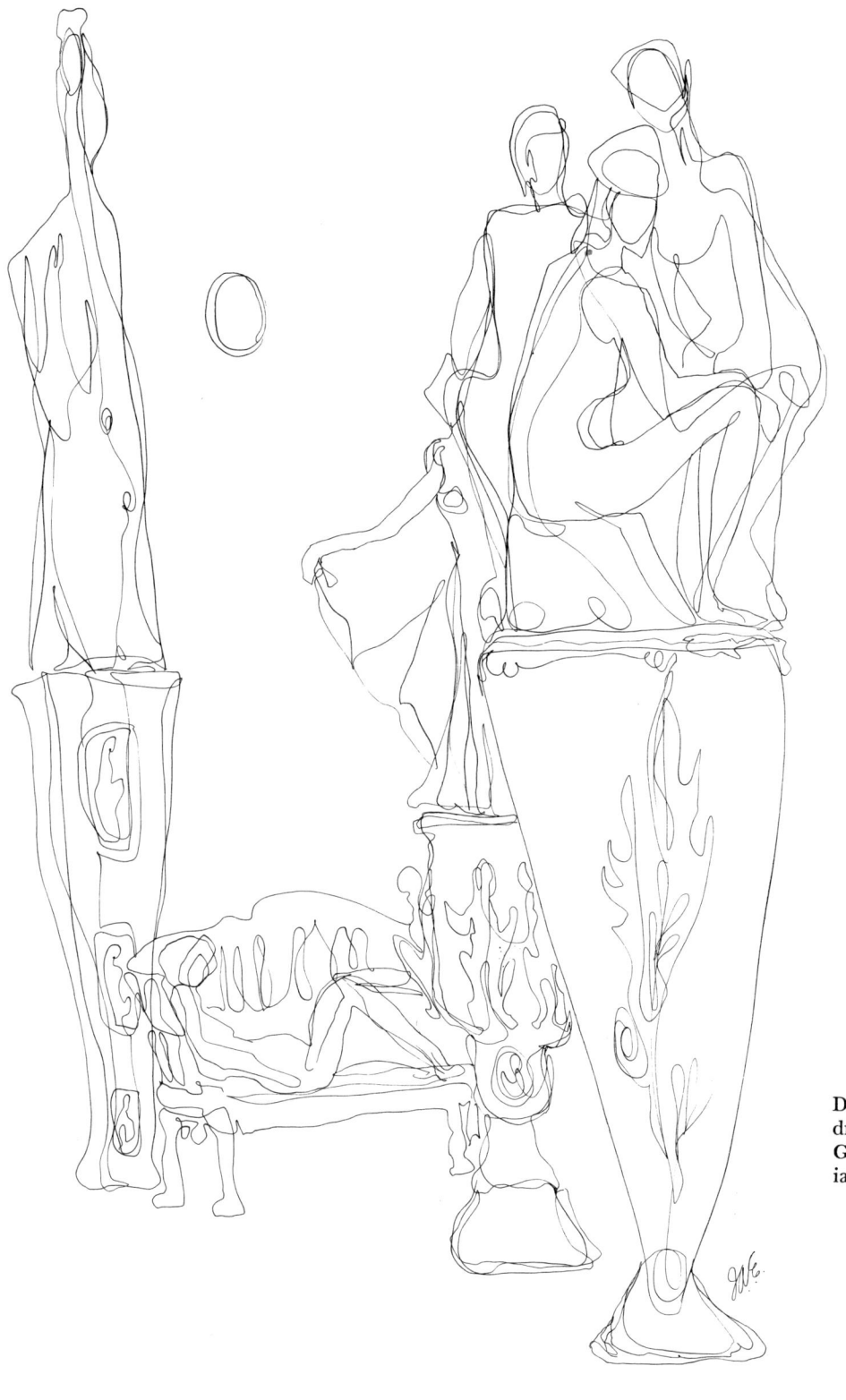

Decorative continuous line drawing on bond pad paper, Gillott pen No. 290. Note variations in line.

the
broken
line

The outline illustrated here suggests continuity but is interrupted by gaps. It is the "stop and go" line, the broken line. It
can be used to give texture or a more aesthetic feel to what would
otherwise be a simple outline. It can also be used as a series of
marks of varying lengths, shapes, and thicknesses to fill in smaller
areas with detail, or to produce the light and shadow which
imply a third dimension.

PEN
AND
INK

Broken line drawing on bond pad paper, Gillott pen No. 170. Note how the broken line suggests details.

Broken line drawing on bond pad paper, Gillott pen No. 290. The broken line produces decorative textural effects.

Broken line drawing on bond pad paper, Esterbrook crow quill pen No. 62.

continuous

and

broken

lines

    These two lines combine well where ornamentation is needed within an area. They lend additional interest to a simple subject. Usually the continuous line is drawn first, then areas are filled in with detail or suggested detail. The combination calls into play all three of the pivot methods: the shoulder pivot for the continuous line, the wrist pivot for more minute work, and the elbow pivot where detail is implied rather than stated.

PEN

AND

INK

Right • Continuous and broken line drawing done on bond pad paper with a Gillott pen No. 290. The broken lines were used for texture and design.

Below • Continuous and broken line drawing on bond pad paper, rendered with a Gillott pen No. 290.

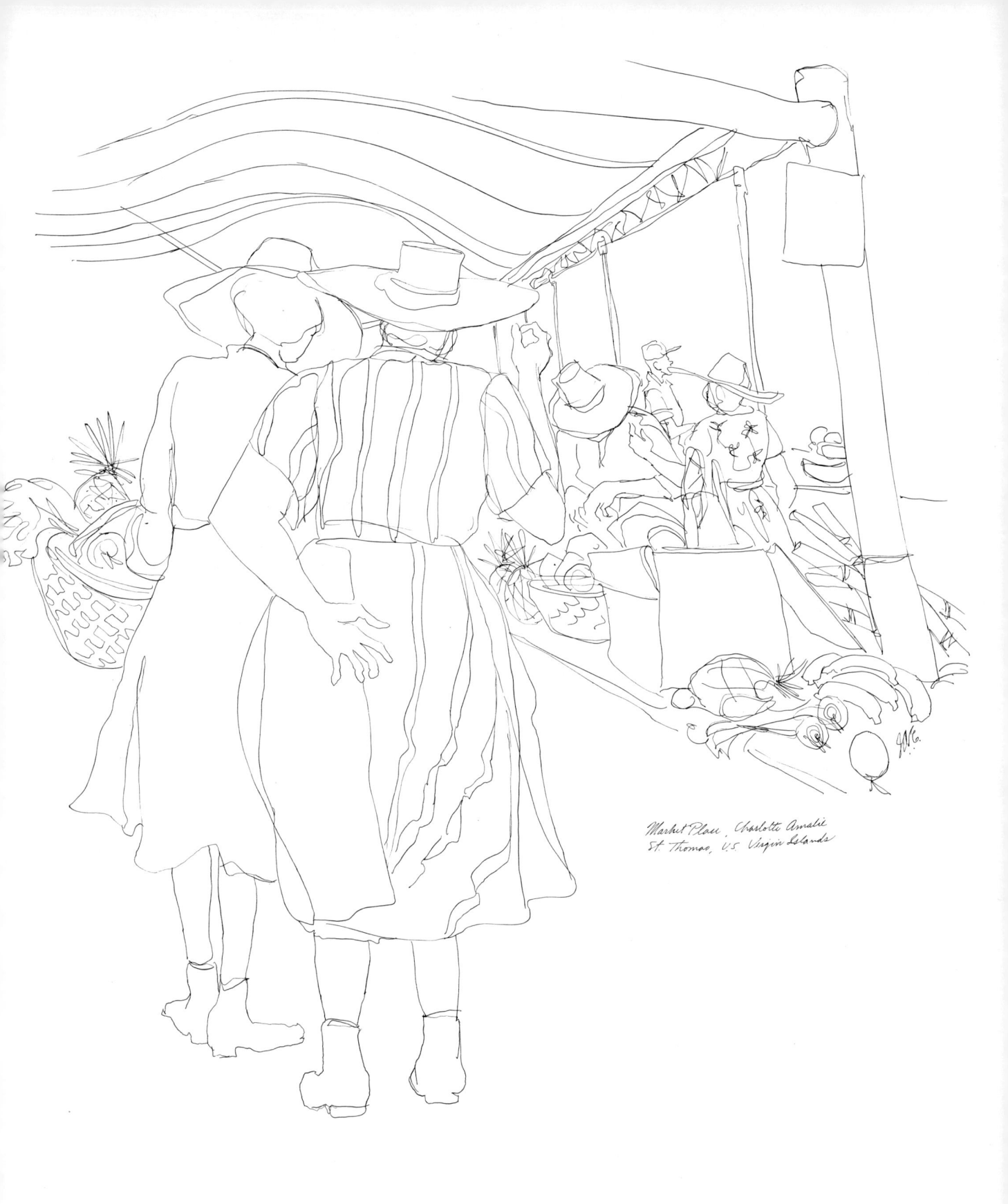

Market Place, Charlotte Amalie
St. Thomas, U.S. Virgin Islands

Above • Continuous and broken line drawing on
bond pad paper, Gillott pen No. 170.

Right • Continuous and broken line drawing on
bond pad paper, Gillott pen No. 290. A very
sensitive line can be achieved with this pen.

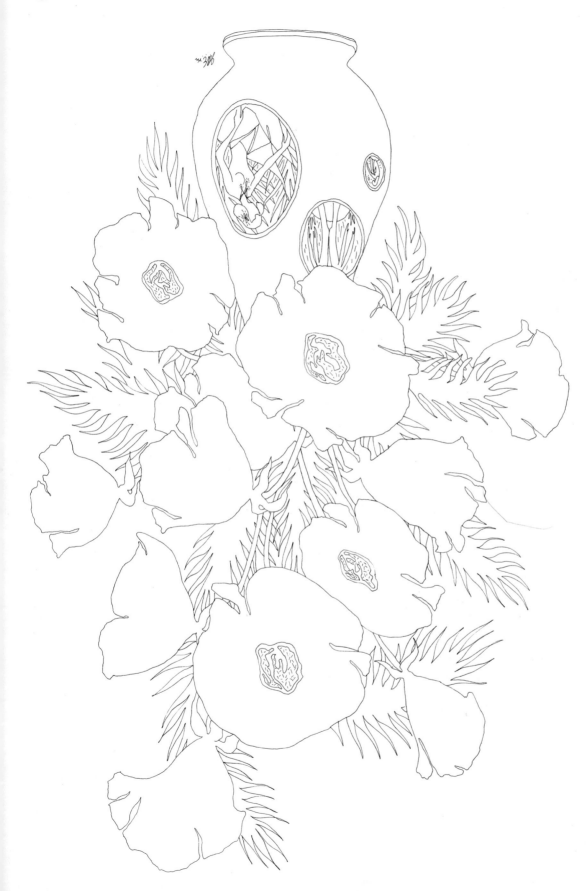

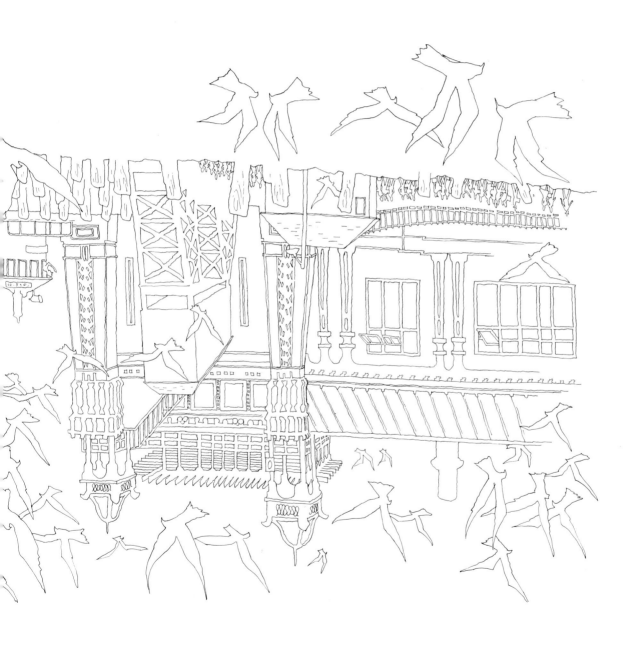

Continuous and broken line drawing
on 3-ply kid finish Strathmore paper,
Gillott pens 170 and 290.

50

Continuous and broken line drawing on 3-ply kid
finish Strathmore paper, Gillott pen No. 290.

the
textured
line

This uneven adaptable line is not a difficult one to master. I look upon it as one of the most comfortable for me. Others may have been using variations, but I found my own interpretation.

For years I had struggled to make the sharp clear lines that were then most in use—straight lines guided with a ruler, or swirling ones aided by a French curve. I found all this not only difficult but frustrating and unsatisfying.

I rebelled, as I am likely to do against the formal, the rigid, the mechanical, and decided to draw lines in my own way. A natural outcome for me was the freer, slightly jagged line which I call the textured line. For fine arts work, it seemed to have a vitality that was lacking in the more geometrically constructed designs. For commercial work, it reduced well photographically and added warmth to a drawing. I enjoyed the line and, needless to say, was pleased when it found acceptance.

The textured line follows a kind of pull-forward-push-back movement, a start-retreat-and-go-again with the retreat at the faintest diagonal. I hold my pen at a slightly greater angle from the vertical than usual, about thirty to forty-five degrees, though this kind of information, I recognize, will vary in usefulness depending upon the individual.

Obviously breath control is unnecessary here due to the nature of the line, as it is usually done with a wrist pivot action such as is used here.

**PEN
AND
INK**

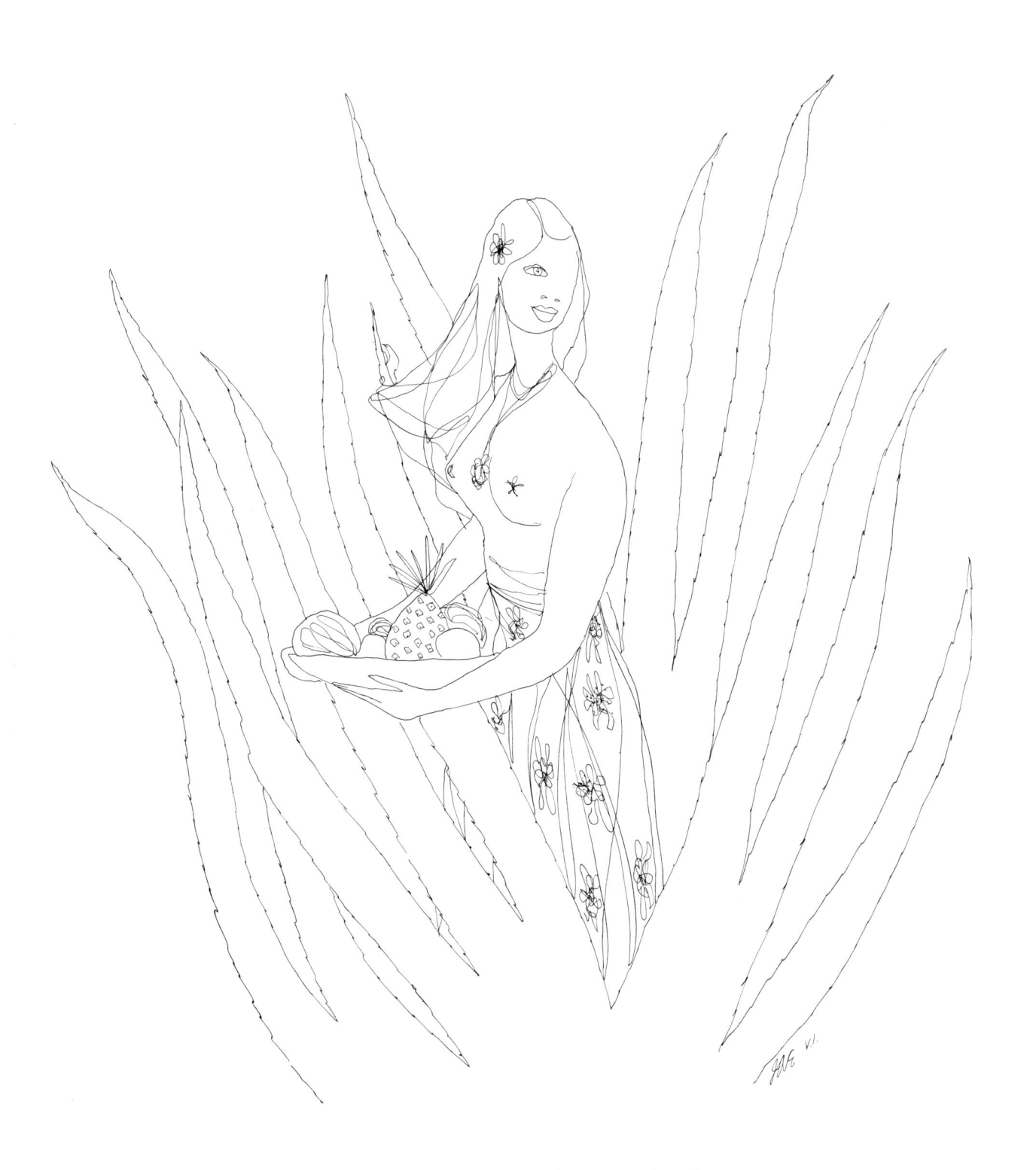

Textured line drawing on bond pad
paper, Gillott pen No. 290.

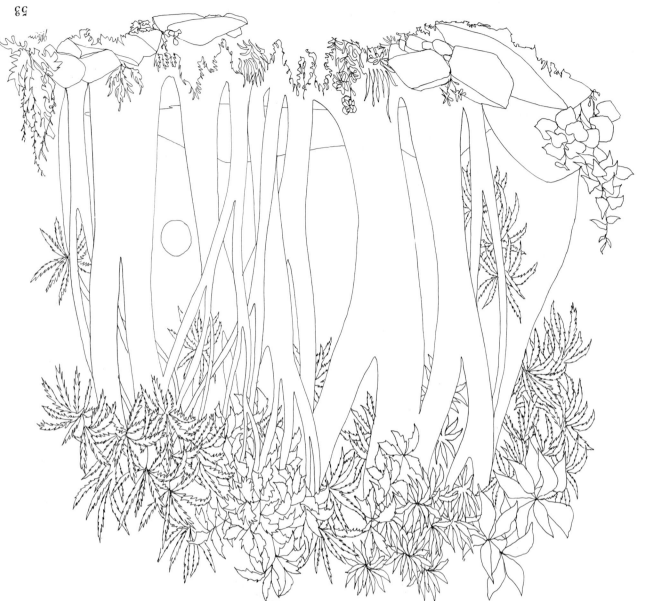

Textured line drawing on bond pad
paper, Gillott pen No. 170.

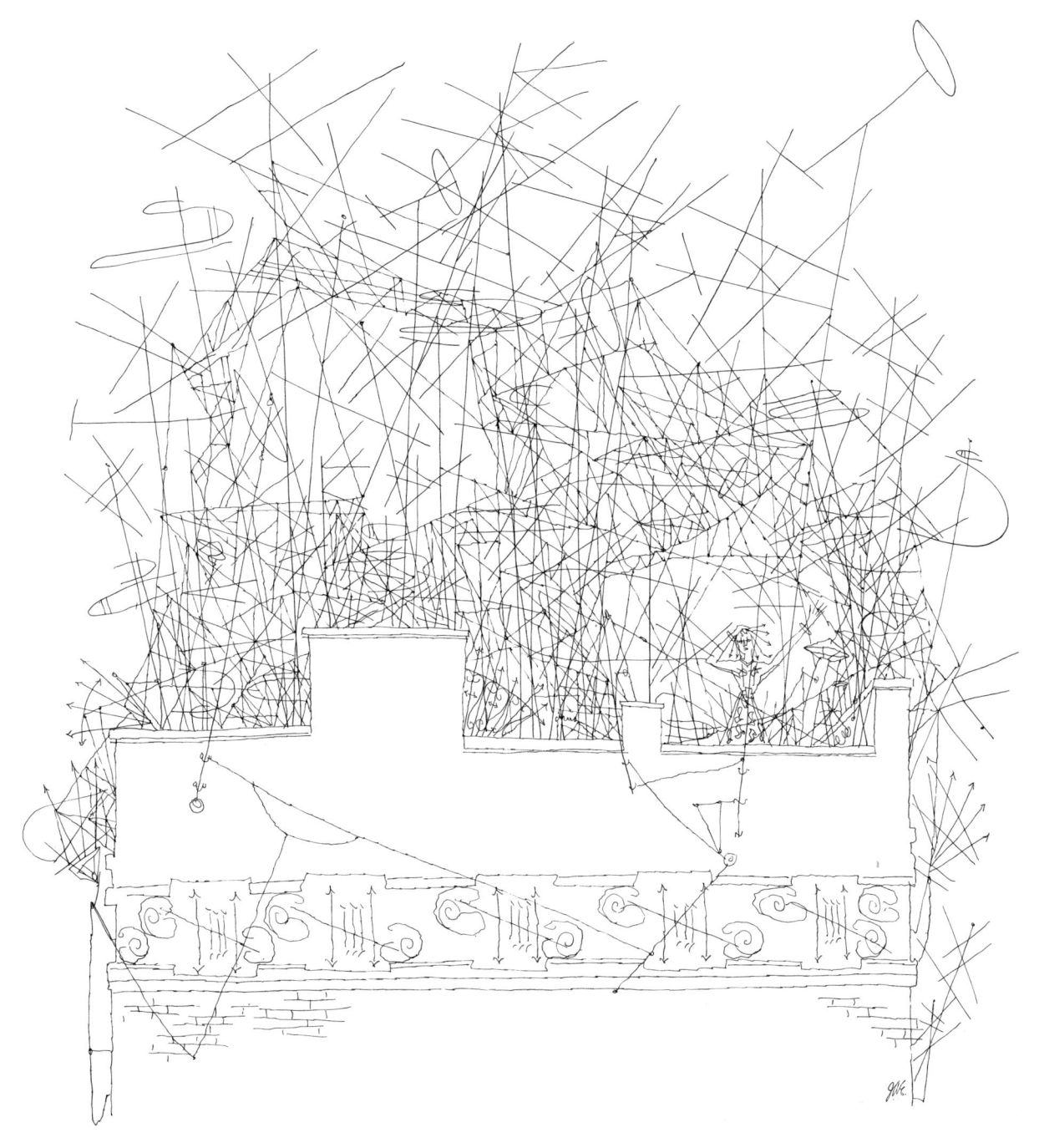

Textured line drawing on bond pad
paper, Gillott pen No. 290.

the
thick
and
thin
line

The control of pressure applied to the pen is the chief factor in drawing the thick-and-thin line; and a pen point of maximum flexibility permits the widest variations.

Points which respond easily for this work are the Esterbrook 355 and the Gillott 290. Either of these will begin with a very fine stroke, and, as it is drawn with pressure across the working surface, will spread readily to a surprisingly broad swathe, and tighten back to fine again. It can be pressed quite hard, to achieve such effects, but obviously if pressed too far, the point will snap. Tests on a scratch sheet are the safest way to gauge maximum spread.

Firmer points, such as are used for heavier line work, will permit some change in breadth of stroke but have nowhere near as wide a span of variation. The firmer they are, the more brittle, and hence faster breaking.

The thin line from the fine point can be made even thinner, depending upon the manner of the pen's use. The sharper the angle from the vertical at which the pen is held, the finer the line. The sideways stroke of the point, dealt with earlier under "The Decorative Continuous Line," will also thin the line.

All three pivot points—shoulder, elbow, and wrist—aid in varying the thick and thin line, though it is with the wrist pivot that one has the greatest control of the pressure on the point.

Thick and thin line drawing on bond
pad paper, Gillott pen No. 290.

Thick and thin line drawing on ledger
pad paper, Gillott pen No. 290.

Thick and thin line drawing on bond pad paper,
Gillott pen No. 290.

combined

pen

lines

Having begun a piece of work in one technique, there is no need for, nor any special virtue in, continuing to completion using that technique only. Combining two or three, or indeed, the whole range of pen lines, can give change of pace, texture, dimension, contrast—unlimited possibilities.

In addition to the textured, the broken, and others already suggested, the dotted line should be mentioned: it is especially effective for decorative notes and for modeling. There is also the familiar and useful cross-hatching.

Perhaps in design work even more than in the realistic approach do combined pen lines come into play, for they offer the artist opportunities for varied effects, unrestricted by the need to be literal. The selections and combinations should be based on the expression and the mood which the artist wants to create.

PEN

AND

INK

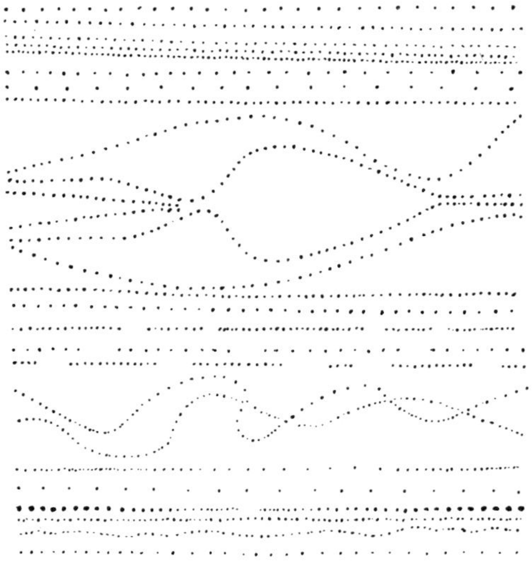

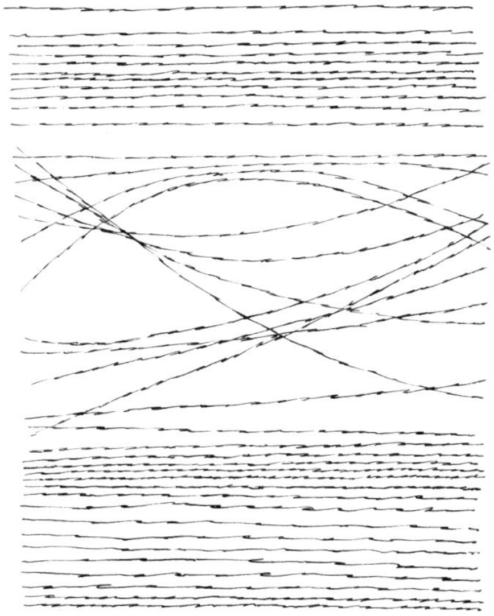

textured line

types
of
pen
lines

curved line

dotted line

straight line

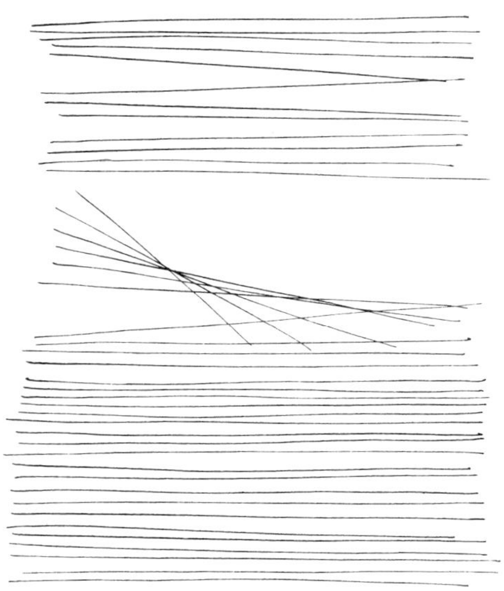

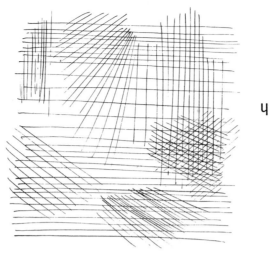

cross hatch

wavy line

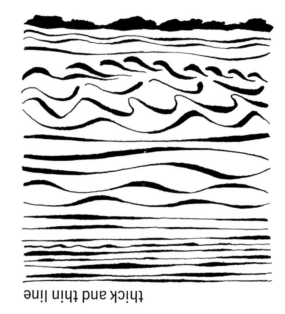

thick and thin line

broken line

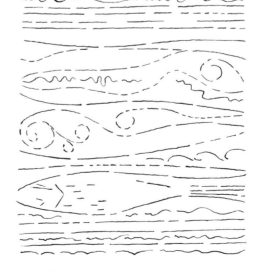

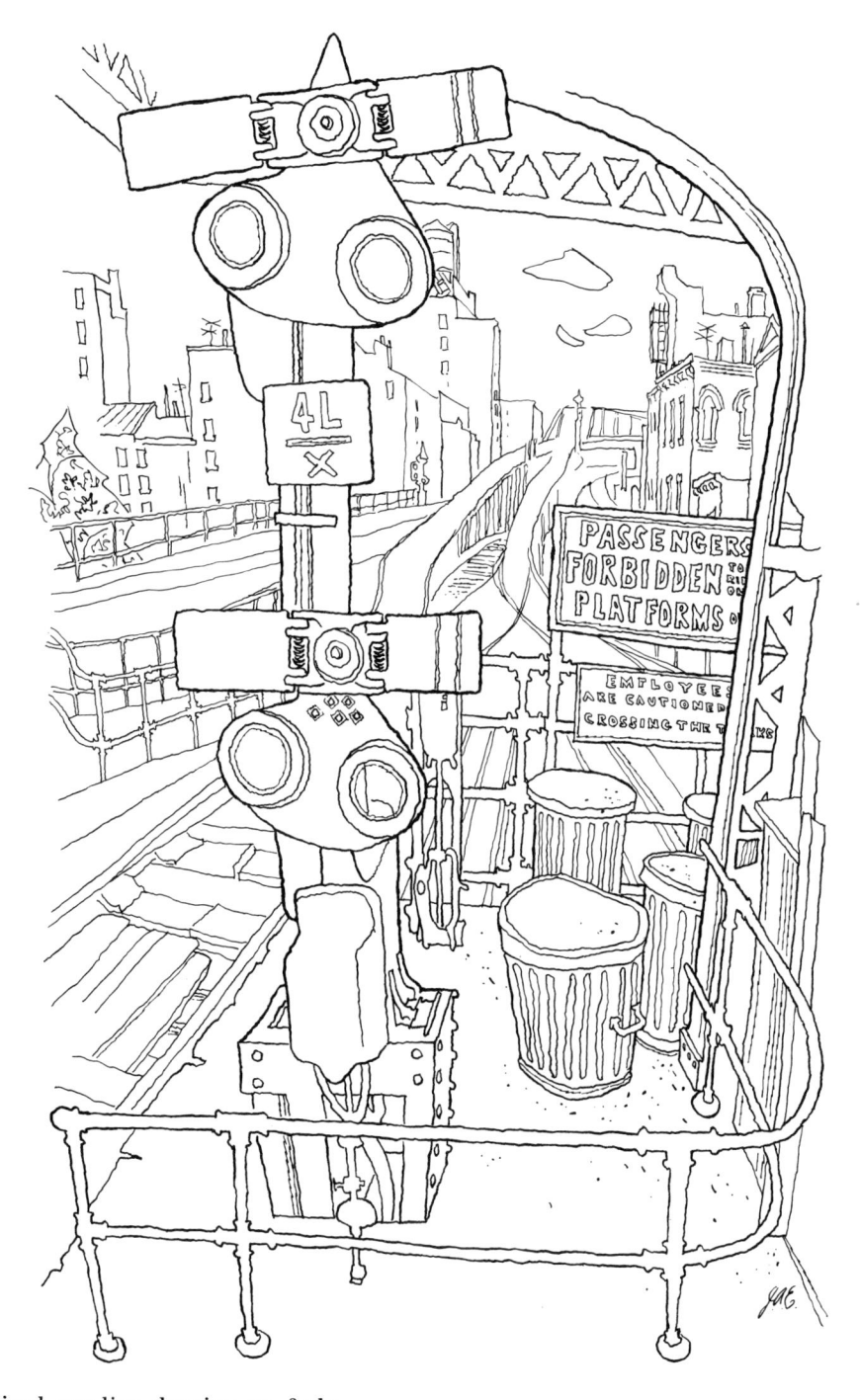

Combined pen-line drawing on 3-ply
kid finish Strathmore paper, Gillott
pen No. 170.

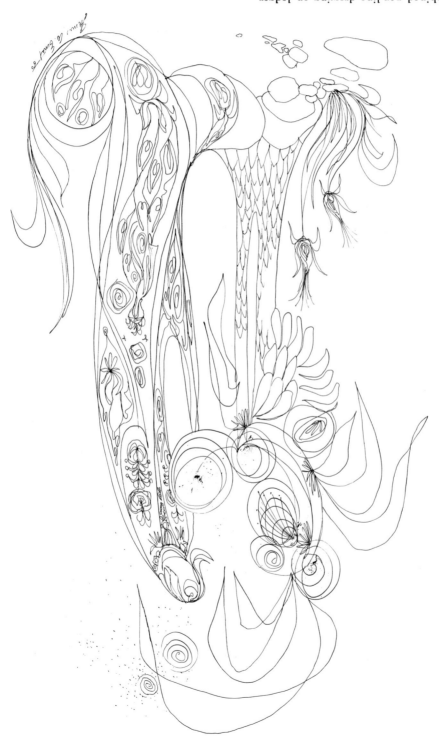

Combined pen-line drawing on ledger pad paper, Gillott pen No. 290.

Right • Combined pen-line drawing on bond pad paper, Esterbrook pen No. 355.

64

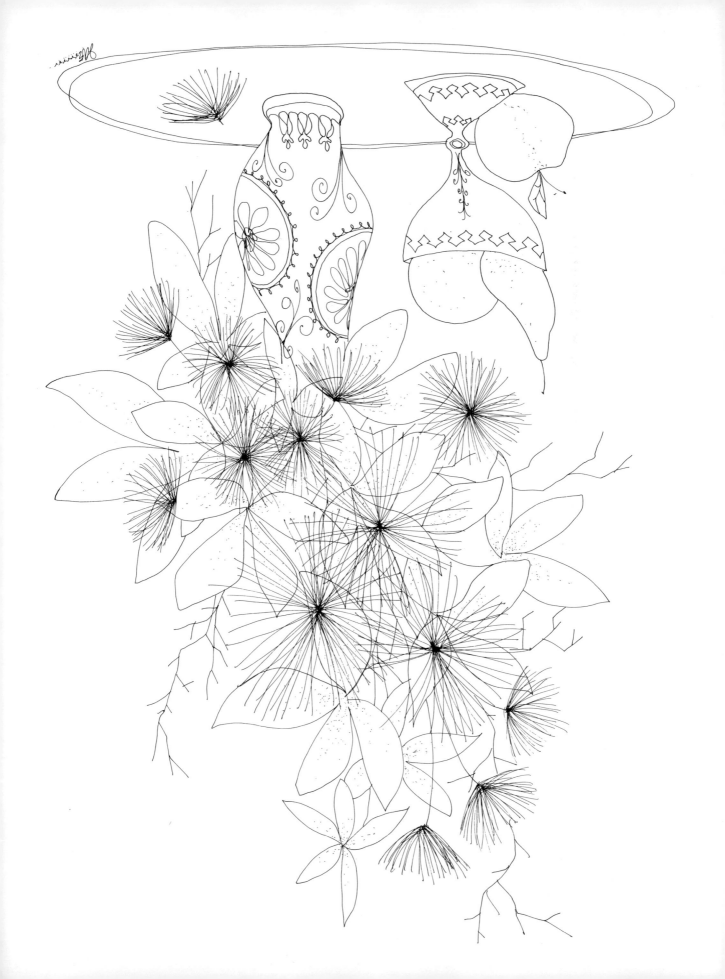

Combined pen-line drawing on 3-ply
kid finish Strathmore paper, Gillott
pen No. 290.

Combined pen-line drawing on 3-ply Kid finish Strathmore paper, Gillott pens No. 170 and 290, and Hunt crow quill pen No. 108.

Combined pen-line drawing done on a blotter and rendered with a Gillott pen No. 290.

Combined pen-line drawing on 3-ply kid finish Strathmore paper, Gillott pens No. 170 and 290.

68

SPECIAL DRAWING PENS

So far, the stroke has been the changing factor in line drawing, the tool remaining basically the same—a pen point in a holder. A new range of effects comes with each change to a different kind of pen, and there are many in the art dealer's stock. Most of them have the advantage of being more portable than a pen and ink bottle, and are ready for service under less favorable circumstances than working in the studio.

I haven't worked with all of them, but I have tried a good many. On those which I have used, let me offer some comment.

The Osmiroid pen is an artist's fountain pen, designed to take India ink. It offers a whole range of interchangeable nibs, including a set for left-handers. I have found it very satisfactory for either sketching or drawing, both in the studio and outside. It is especially handy for travel.

The Ball Point India ink pen operates with a replaceable cartridge. It gives a fairly even line, but of course has no flexibility. It works well for outline drawing and more precise work, but, for me at least, any ball point pen lacks real character of line.

The Rapidograph is a type of fountain pen with an even weight of line which is especially good for technical drawings. Its interchangeable nibs come in different sizes and shapes, and the holder carries a refillable ink cartridge. The pen is used extensively in mechanicals for commercial art. It has been my bad luck to have it clog, though it is not supposed to do so.

The Rapidoball is a mechanical variation of the Rapidograph, for much the same use. I have found no working difference between the two.

The Perlon brush-tipped fountain pen has replaceable brush nibs, which come either round or flat and in assorted sizes, for drawing and lettering. My use of it has been chiefly for layout work.

The Bamboo pen is, literally, cut from bamboo, and is used more or less as a penholder with a pen point would be. It is not a fountain pen, but a reed which must be dipped in ink. I have found it an interesting pen to draw with for unusual effects, particularly on rice paper.

The Pelican Graphos is another of the fountain pens for technical work, with a variety of nibs, used mostly for lettering, graphs, and such.

The Cado Flo-Master is an example of the felt-tip pen. It uses a special fluid instead of the usual drawing ink and is refillable. The five nibs available range from $\frac{1}{8}$ to $\frac{1}{4}$ inch in size, and in shape are round or square with "bullet," chisel, or other type points.

These pens operate on a saturation principle. To start the flow, one holds the pen vertically and presses down until the spongy felt of the nib absorbs some of the fluid. A limited absorption will give a light hazy line. Further and repeated pressure on the nib changes the value, grading up to a sharp rich black.

My preference has been for the round, thinner felts—the Number 10 bullet-shaped, or the finer Number 1. With these tips, a line can always be widened, whereas the broader felts make a thin line impossible. I use this pen more than any other of its type for layout and rendering work. The felt-tip nib does wear down, and it is well always to keep a spare on hand. Lacking a replacement, however, one can restore the nib by sharpening it with sandpaper. Indeed, it is possible to change the shape of a nib with sandpaper and develop any preferred type of point. This takes time and careful work, but it can be done.

Miracle Markers, Magic Markers, and Dri-Mark are also felt-tip tools, all with more or less the same general characteristics. They are used widely in advertising work for layout, rendering, and lettering. The Miracle Markers have worked well for me since the nibs are slightly smaller and the fluid has the quality of maintaining an outline without spreading.

the
felt-
tip
line

The versatile felt-tip pen has a character of its own which cannot be attained with any other tool. Its line is as different from others as the quality of felt differs from the quality of metal. Excellent for sketching and drawing, it can, with the same tip, give a strong black stroke or a soft, sensitive line. Though its interchangeable nibs are limited in number, they are seemingly unlimited in the variety of work they will accomplish.

The felt-tip is truly an artist's pen—an all-purpose pen. It gives vitality and variety for fast sketching on location; equally it provides satisfying effects for finished work, and it "takes" well on almost any surface.

I find the Cado Flo-Master especially satisfactory for travel. As a matter of fact, it is one pen which I am never without, and, to go farther with this admission, I am rarely without two of them, equipped with my two favorite tips and ready for action.

SPECIAL

DRAWING

PENS

Felt-tip pen drawing on bond pad paper, Flo-Master pen with No. 1 nib.

Felt-tip pen drawing on 3-ply kid finish Strathmore paper, Flo-Master pen with No. 1 nib.

Felt-tip pen drawing on canvas paper,
Flo-Master pen and No. 1 nib.

Felt-tip pen drawing on bond pad paper, Flo-Master pen and No. 10 nib.

Variations with brush and Rich Art poster paint.
The frontispiece is an example of this technique.

BRUSH WITH INK OR PAINT

Line drawings made with a brush bring into first consideration the tools and materials to be used, as was the case with pen drawings.

Brushes are of three general types—the round or pointed, the oval, and the flat-tipped or chisel-edged—and sizes range from the very small to the comparatively large. There are also various kinds of brush hairs. Horse hair, camel hair, and sable are all soft brushes, with sable hair the finest. Bristle brushes are not likely to be used for line work.

Winsor & Newton sable brushes (and I consider Series 7 the finest of the line) last long and survive hard use. Grumbacher brushes are also excellent. The make, the type, the size and shape of brushes are all choices to be made on the basis of the artist's experiment and preference.

Keeping separate brushes for paint and for ink is an aid to good work and to the preservation of these tools. It is necessary to speak briefly of the importance of cleaning them after each use. The ink brushes need soapy water worked into them thoroughly, while water rinsing should be sufficient to clear away the water-soluble paints. For drying, brushes should be flicked to a point, chisel-edge, or whatever, so that the hairs fall back into place to maintain the brushes' original shape.

The hairs must be protected also when brushes are being packed or carried—either mask-taped to a cardboard or rolled in paper jackets extending beyond the brush tips.

The black paints for which I have formed a preference are Rich Art poster paint and Winsor & Newton Designers' Opaque. The inks I use for brush are the same as for pen—Higgins India Ink and Pelikan Opaque. There are many other good varieties.

Experimenting with the many surfaces and textures possible for line drawing is limited only by the artist's imagination and

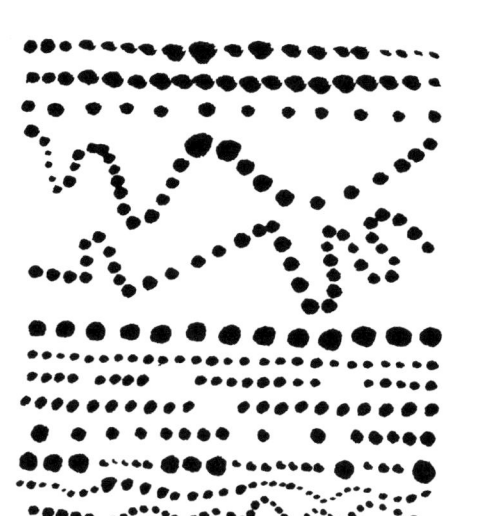

split brush line

dotted line

crisp line

types
of
brush
lines

wavy line

thick-and-thin line

textured line

dry brush line

broken line

ingenuity. There is, of course, great variety in drawing papers and illustration boards. There are also various other surfaces which give interesting and original and satisfying effects—all kinds of mounting boards, window shade cloth (yes, the roller curtains!), burlap and the various fibre cloths, fabrics of plain color or white, sailcloth, wood, the grey soft-surface shirt-boards that come from the laundry, anything with texture or grain, and, at the other end of the range, acetate.

Such a diversity of tools and materials invites the artist to adapt a variety of techniques. Some of these are set forth here.

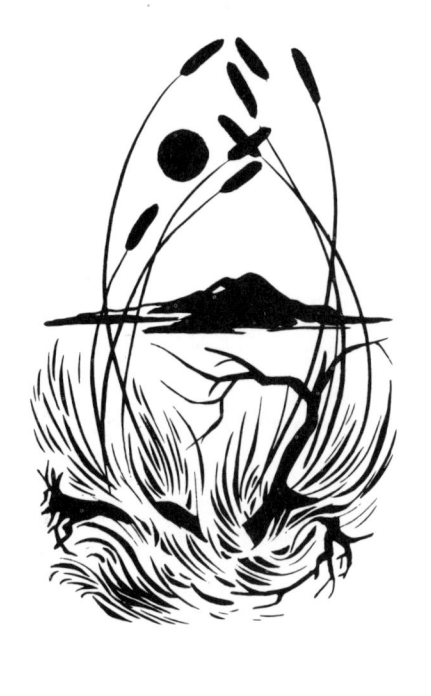

the

crisp

line

Deft, sure strokes make the crisp line, with side edges clean and sharp. There are usually variations in weight of line, however, due to the character of brush work.

When paint is used, the crisp brush line works better on a smooth surface. With ink, the texture is less important since the consistency of ink allows ease of flow on all surfaces.

It is possible, however, to achieve a crisp line with paint on textured surfaces, if the paint is thinned with water slightly more than usual to enable it to work into the texture. Paint will keep its black, whereas ink, for which thinning is not only unnecessary but inadvisable, will lose out to a greyish tone.

For paper, my choices have been Strathmore Kid-finish, Whatman medium surface, bond pad, or ledger pad.

BRUSH

WITH

INK

OR

PAINT

The crisp brush line on 3-ply plate-finish Strathmore paper, rendered in ink.

the

dry

brush

line

Ink and paint work equally well for the dry brush line; and as for paper surface, the choice of texture depends upon what the artist wants his finished expression to be.

With ink, the brush is dipped and then twirled on a scratch sheet until only a very little ink remains. The brush is then ready for the stroke. I can describe the action in no other way than that one "drags" the brush across the paper to produce the rather shaggy, uneven line.

With paint, very little water—sometimes almost no water—is used. The brush can work directly from the paint container to the paper for the dry line.

BRUSH

WITH

INK

OR

PAINT

Dry brush drawing on rice paper, rendered in ink
with a Japanese bamboo brush.

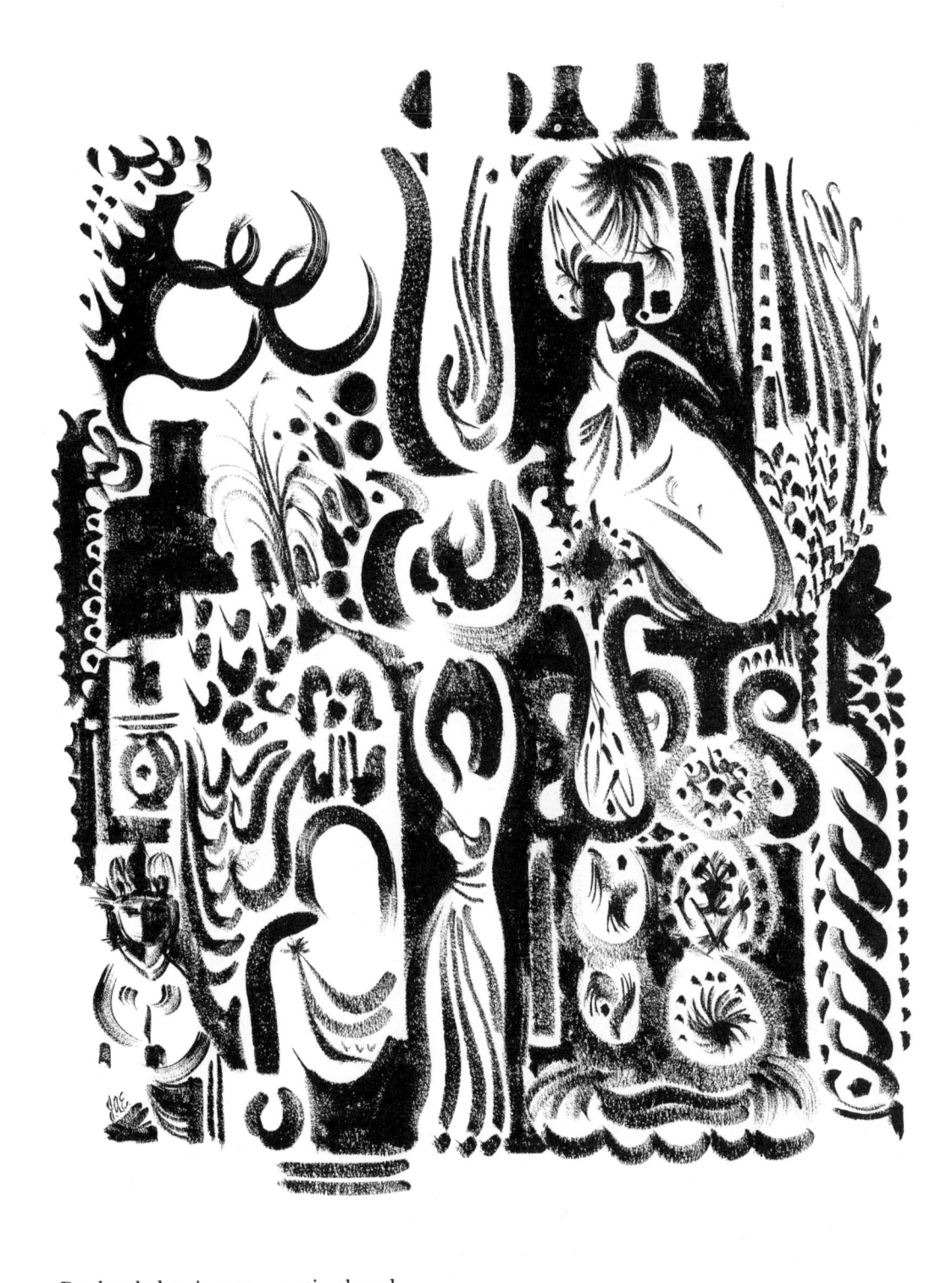

Dry brush drawing on mounting board,
done with poster paint.

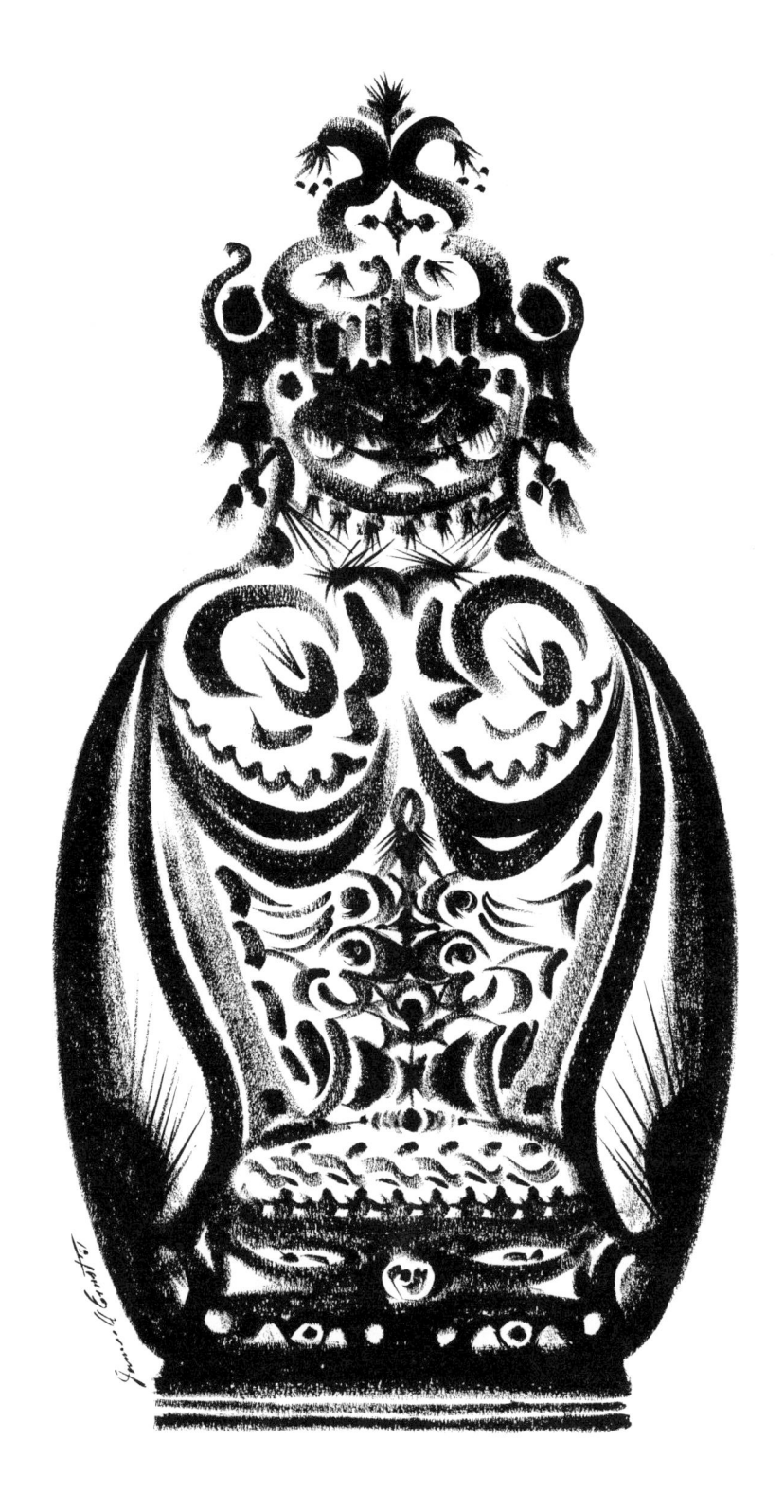

Dry brush drawing on mounting board,
Rich Art poster paint.

the

split

brush

line

Working the split-brush line successfully comes only after considerable practice. This line is used less often by itself than in conjunction with other lines.

   Medium textured or smooth surfaces seem best. The ink or paint is handled very much as in the dry-brush line. The brush is worked fairly dry first. Then pressure divides the brush hairs into two or more parts. The scratch pad is the place to find the split that offers the most interesting possibilities.

   Paint, as before, is thinned only very slightly, just enough for the medium to give some firmness and cohesion to the divided brush hairs. With ink, the time elapsed in making the trial lines usually allows the fluid to dry to the degree needed to hold the split hairs in position. As must be apparent, it is the preliminary trials which provide this technique with individuality in results.

BRUSH

WITH

INK

OR

PAINT

Split-brush drawing on 3-ply kid finish Strathmore paper, Rich Art poster paint.

the

broken

line

Any of the brush strokes presented so far may be drawn as a broken line. The use here is similar to that of the interrupted pen line illustrated previously—for suggested outline, for texture, for detail, for light and shadow. The round brush with its pointed tip can give a series of softer lines with tapered ends, while the chisel-edge brush offers more staccato effect. The length of line between gaps may be stretched to a degree which suggests sketching, or shortened almost to dots.

BRUSH

WITH

INK

OR

PAINT

89

Right • Broken-line design on 3-ply kid finish Strathmore paper, Rich Art poster paint. Note the simple, direct brush strokes.

Below • Broken-line ink drawing on bond pad paper. Note the various kinds of brush strokes.

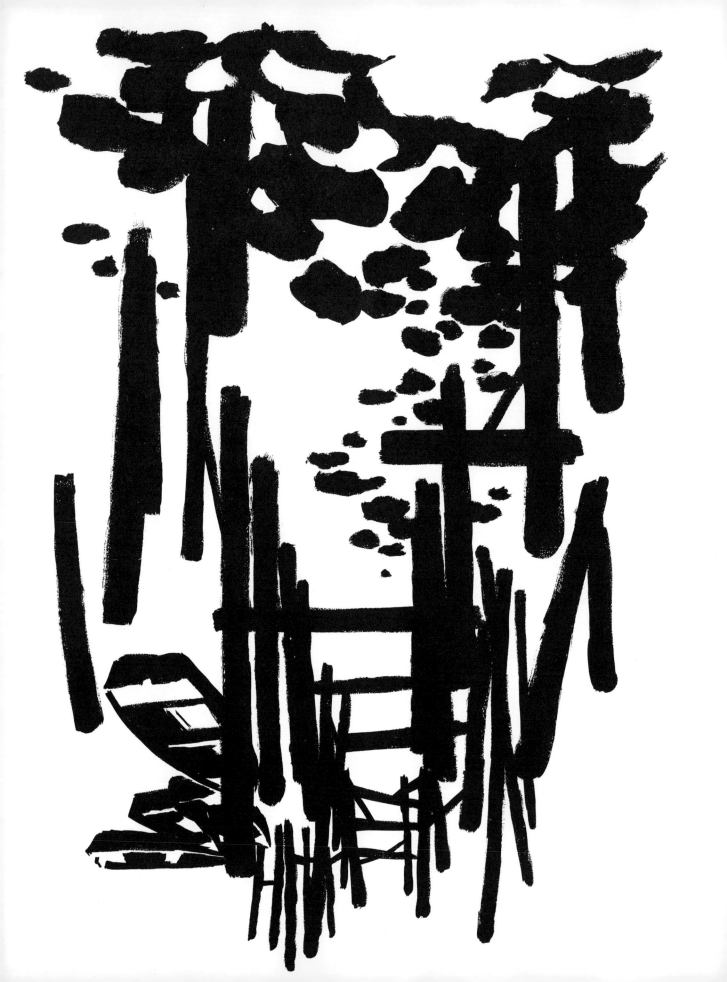

Broken-line drawing on bond pad paper, Rich Art poster paint. Vertical lines are used throughout.

PEN AND BRUSH COMBINED

Combinations of types of lines are often the seasoning which adds zest to a drawing. Of these, one flavor can be brought out above others by the change to a different tool. The addition of pen lines to brush work may develop a competent enough drawing into one of far superior interest.

In the integration of these two, however, one should be mindful of the importance of maintaining unequal proportions. The work should be a brush drawing with pen added, or a pen and ink piece with brush accents, one supporting the other, rather than competing.

There must also be some thought as to the compatibility of lines. Heavy brush strokes or large solid areas may overpower the pen work.

A pen drawing is at its best when it is not too large. Even though brush drawings can be less limited in size, the combination of the two must stay within bounds or the pen work will be lost. At a guess, seventeen by twenty-four inches is about as large as such work should be if the pen work is to keep its significance. A medium-textured surface seems best adapted for the interplay of these two techniques.

The artist's own idea will suggest the best possibilities for expression. He may want a bold shaggy brush outline, with pen filling in detail. Or, for a feeling of openness, he may draw in pen and ink, with emphasis in brush.

This seems as good an opportunity as any to offer a general comment on the use of varied lines. Though the range of combinations, both as to technique and tool is almost infinite, the mere grouping of assorted strokes is without merit. The artist who has practiced enough to cultivate an easy familiarity with all these lines is the one who will be best able to call upon the ones he needs to convey on paper the idea in his mind. Variation is important, then, only as it serves this purpose.

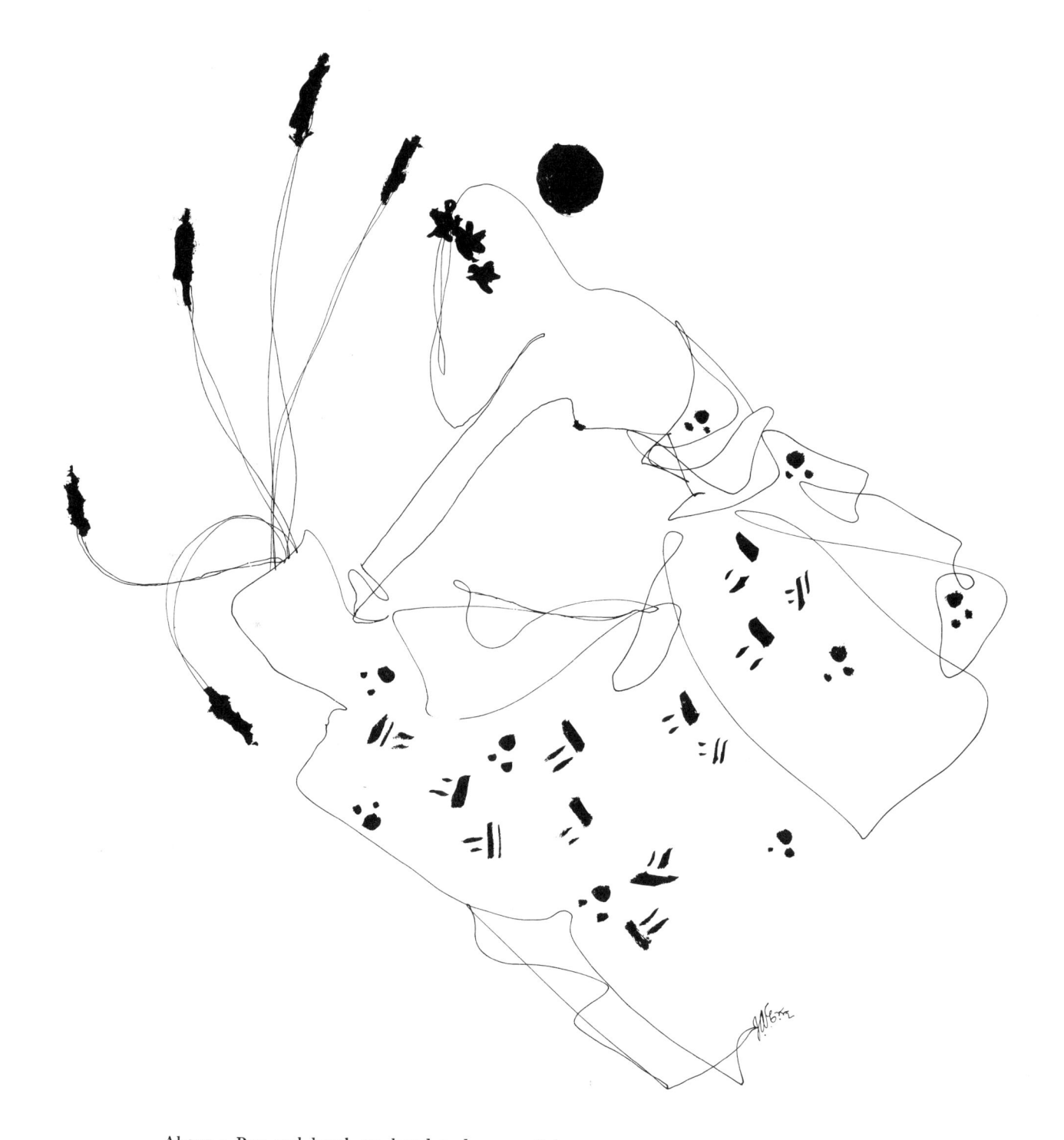

Above • Pen and brush on bond pad paper. Ink was used for both pen, Gillott 170, and brush. Here is the continuous line with brush marks used only as accents.

Right • Pen and brush drawing on mounting board, Rich Art poster black and a Gillott pen No. 290. Note the bold brush design detailed with pen work.

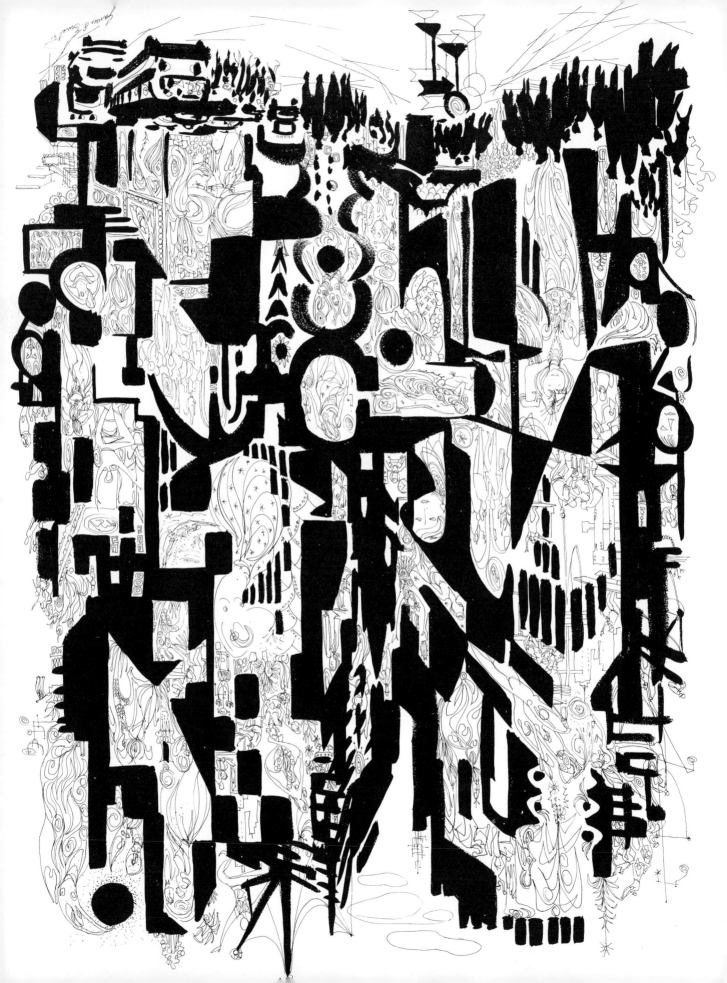

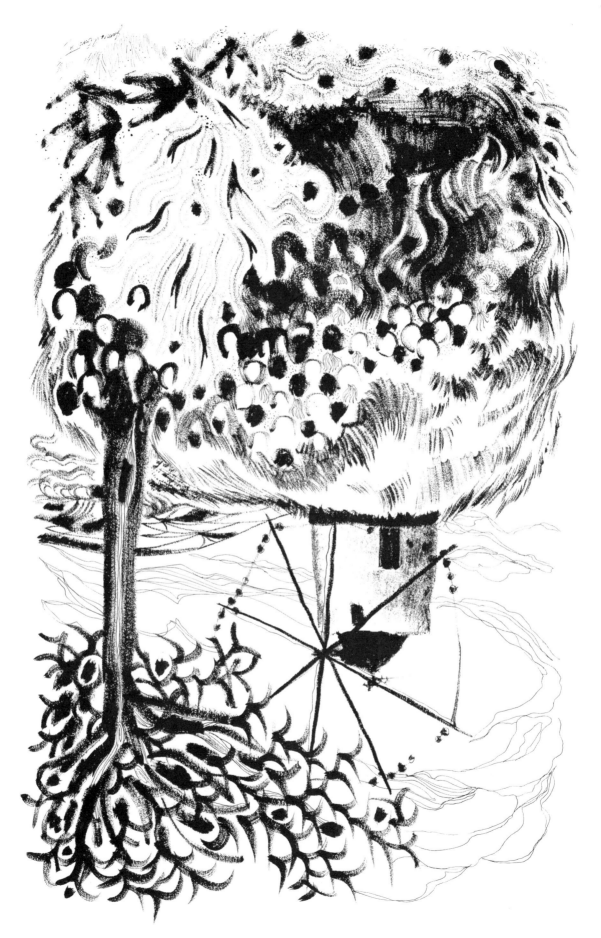

Above • Pen and brush ink drawing on canvas paper. Accents were added with a Gillott pen No. 290.

Left • Pen and brush drawing on special mounting board, ink and paint. Gillott 290 and 170 give pen accents.

Pen and brush drawing on 3-ply kid finish Strathmore paper. Pen work was done with a Gillott pen No. 290 and the brush was used for accents.

ERRORS AND CORRECTIONS

There is an old saying that "putty and paint cover a multitude of sins." There is not likely to be any putty in the line man's kit of tools, but paint certainly plays a part in covering sins—or errors.

In the commercial art field, a wrong line or a change of mind can be taken care of, not so easily to be sure, but it can be done. White poster paint will cover a black line so that a different stroke can be made over it. The trick is to cover the black line successfully, so that it doesn't show through, yet not to allow the white paint to "pile up" too thickly. The several poster whites include Rich Art, Artone, and Shiva, all of which I have used, but my current favorite is Dr. Martin's Homogenized. It really is a "bleed-proof" white.

For more drastic changes, the incorrect area can be re-drawn on another sheet and rubber-cemented as a patch over the original work. With board, the surface of the incorrect area should be stripped off and the patch, similarly stripped, fitted in as a mosaic. When the original art is photographed for the final work of printing, the errors will have disappeared.

So far, this chapter does not apply to the fine artist. For him, no patches are possible, since it is his original work which is significant. His ability is represented in his getting a stroke right the first time, in seeing that every line he sets forth contributes to conveying his thought. If an area doesn't come out right, he practices some more on a scratch pad and starts again.

Until Utopia, however, no doubt we shall still make occasional slips, the pen will still catch in the paper and spatter, the ink will have sediment, the point will snap. For these hazards, there are methods of minor surgery.

Top-ranking is the eraser—a *clean* white round typewriter

eraser, such as the Weldon Roberts 900 Suede, or any medium-soft eraser for ink or paint. In conjunction with this, a typewriter erasing shield protects the area around the error. A Nodalon, art gum, or kneaded eraser will smooth the surface disturbed by the ink eraser and prepare it for the ink or paint again.

Other erasers which do a good job and have their own advantages are the Eberhard Faber Van Dyke, a soft ink eraser; the stick type eraser such as the Blaisdell, paper-covered and resembling a pencil; the Rush Fybrglass propel-repel brush; the electric eraser (a word of caution, here, on the danger of burning too much into the surface).

Of course, many artists prefer a razor blade or sharp knife, X-Acto or other, to any eraser for removing ink or paint.

If preliminary pencil marks are made on the paper prior to inking, they must be removed with care. Any eraser will remove lead pencil, but if rubbed carelessly over the drawing, the eraser will very likely remove a little of the ink also, greying slightly what had been clear black. I have concluded that the Nodalon vinyl eraser called "Miracle" is well named. I find it the very best for cleaning a drawing without greying in the least the pen or brush lines.

Any artist who does much pencil work has his favorite eraser, perhaps most often a kneaded eraser. Kohplastic No. 10 is one of these, or A. W. Faber's Castell Plastic Eraser No. 7530. Others reach for an art gum, unless, like me, they prefer the Nodalon. Quite a different type is the Eberhard Faber Union, with one end for pencil and the other for ink.

When using tools other than lead pencils—charcoal, pastel, carbon, or the grease pencils—the artist will wish he hadn't made the mistake in the first place! Errors are very difficult to remove and they require, in addition to the best erasers available, *pa-*

tience. A kneaded or similar eraser will clear off the surface substance. Then a more abrasive eraser must be worked carefully and patiently, and the paper or board smoothed again.

Erasers are indispensable tools for the artists—or for almost anyone else, for that matter—and are among the least expensive items in his whole equipment. It is for other than economic reasons, then, that it may be said, the better the artist, the longer lasting his eraser. The very best method for extending the life of an artist's eraser is—practice.

Brush and ink drawing on rice paper. For commercial
work corrections can be made with white paint even
though they will show because of the texture of rice
paper. For fine arts work it would be best to start over.

PENCILS
STICKS
AND
CRAYONS

LEAD
CARBON
LITHOGRAPHIC
GREASE
WAX
CHARCOAL
PASTEL

Every type of pencil has its own distinct character. And every pencil, when applied to different textures, produces its own variations of that character.

Many sketching and drawing pencils, crayon, pastel, and others come in one grade only, with no range from hard to soft. Lead pencils, however, usually work in both directions, from a hybrid medium, HB, through progressively harder ones, up to 9H, Hard, and through progressively softer ones down to 6B. The brands most familiar to me are Venus, Eagle Turquoise, Van Dyke michrotone, and Kohinoor. Two, among others, which use a different system of grading are Mongol and Hardmuth Negro

pencils; these use numbers 1, 2, 3, etc., to designate degree of hardness.

The harder pencils are generally used for exacting tasks like drafting or tracing, and also for final drawing prior to ink or paint. The drawing surface has a lot to do with the degree of hardness to be employed, for hard pencils have an unfortunate way of biting in, if one is not careful.

When soft pencils are used on a drawing before inking, a kneaded eraser should lighten the line as much as is practicable, removing excess particles of lead. Otherwise, the flow of ink or paint will be uneven over the lead deposit.

When the finished art work is to be a pencil drawing, the selection of pencils and surfaces becomes even more important. These are detailed further under individual headings in subsequent pages.

Textured working surfaces can be used to advantage in pencil line drawing. Ross drawing boards come in wide variety, as do Coquille stippled boards, Bainbridge Coquille, Whatman, Strathmore, and many others.

Fixative is important to keep pencil work clean and free from smudging. The push-button spray-can should be held some twelve inches above the drawing and in such a position as to allow the spray to fall vertically on it. This helps to avoid the problem of spreading excess particles and thus thickening the lines.

I spray a very light coat of fixative first; then, after allowing it to dry, spray thoroughly. The softer the pencil, the more care is needed in fixing. Two types which I have used satisfactorily are Blair "Spray-fix" and Eagle "Fixatif," and also occasionally, "Krylon."

the

lead

pencil

line

Of the common or doodling variety of lead pencil, I lean towards the soft, the degree depending upon the job to be done. For preliminary sketching, I work with a 2B, up to even a 6B; when I have resolved the drawing and am ready for the finished work, I might use a 3H to trace down the drawing; for the finish, I choose HB to 6B. This last phase, however, is where the artist's individual choice is most significant.

I like to make my own transfer sheet. I blacken a piece of tracing paper with a 6B pencil, then go over this pencilled surface *once* (never retracing) with a wad of cotton moistened lightly with rubber cement thinner. This reduces the danger of smudge when the transfer sheet is placed on the final paper for tracing.

Even after the careful selection of the right pencil is made, an artist may wish, as I do, to individualize his tool even further. I use a sandpaper pad to fashion the exact shape of point I want, whether it be stiletto-sharp, a blunt flat edge, or some other style.

PENCILS

STICKS

AND

CRAYONS

Lead pencil drawing on bond pad paper, 6B Venus pencil. Note the broken lines.

Lead pencil drawing on mimeograph paper, HB Eagle pencil. Drawn on location with some areas in detail and others suggested. Such a drawing is sometimes used as a preliminary sketch.

Following page • Lead pencil drawing on 3-ply kid finish Strathmore paper. Eagle Turquoise pencils HB through 6B were used. Note broken-line variety and arrangement.

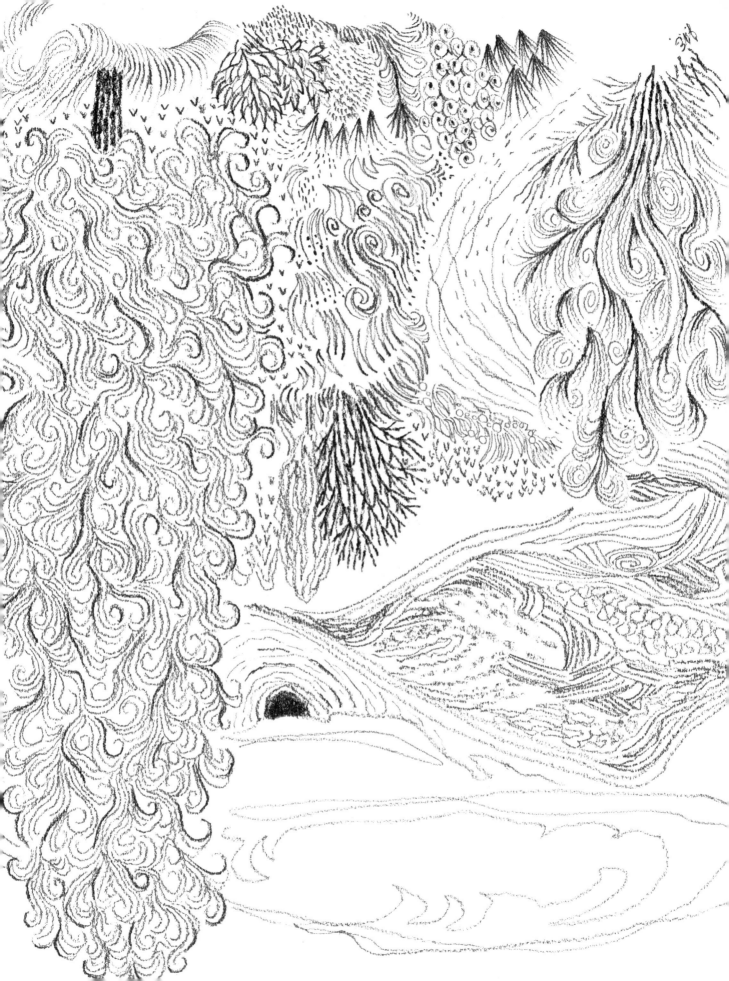

the
carbon
pencil
line

The carbon pencil offers a richer quality of black than does the lead pencil. I use this type frequently for comprehensive sketches in commercial art, usually choosing a Wolff B, BB, or BBB, and regular bond drawing paper.

Again, as in all line work, the character of line depends not only on the pencil used, but on the selection of working surface. I like the bond paper, but when I happen to want a change of texture, I put a textured board under the sheet on which I am working. It does very well.

PENCILS
STICKS
AND
CRAYONS

Carbon pencil drawing on 3-ply kid finish Strathmore paper, Wolff HB, BB, and BBB pencils. Note the texture and types of lines.

the
lithographic
grease
or
wax
pencil
line

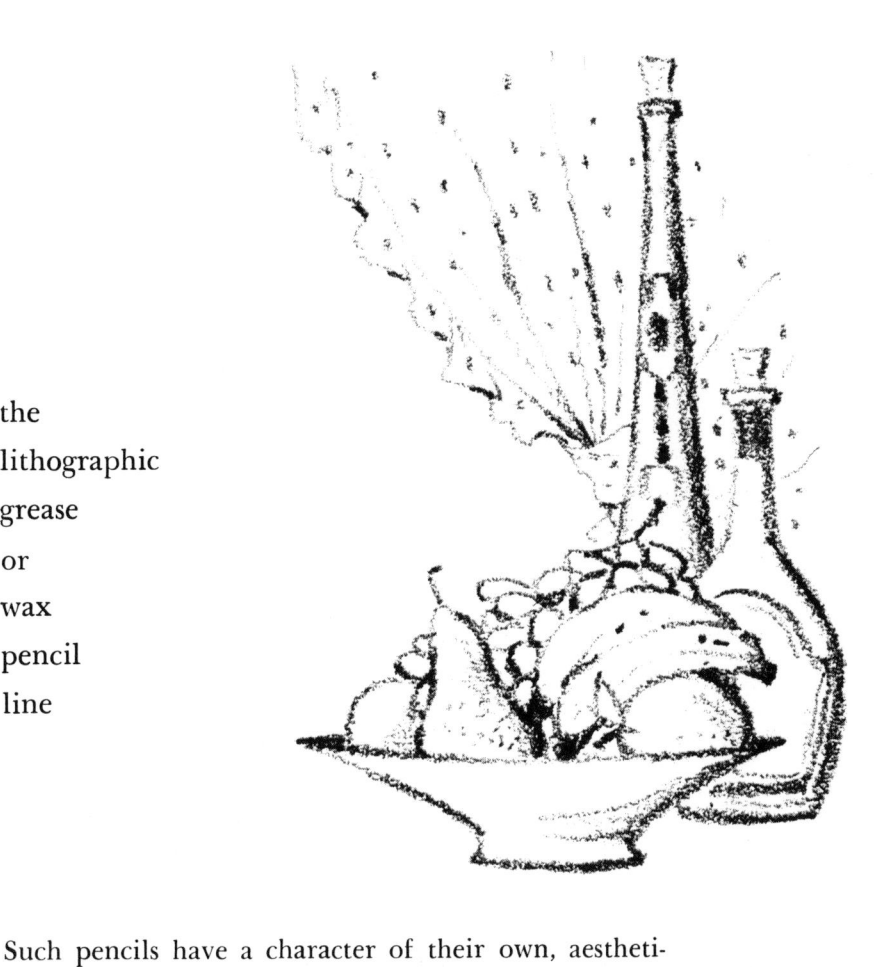

Such pencils have a character of their own, aesthetically. By the nature of their base ingredient, they offer the additional practical advantage of working as well on plastic, glass, metal, etc., as they do on the usual paper and boards.

The range of tools here includes the china-marking pencils, jumbo wax easel crayons, lithographic crayons, and others. The Conté crayon pencil in sanguine is a pleasure to use. My preference runs to Korn's lithographic crayon pencils and the Blaisdell china-marking pencils. All of them, especially the lithographic pencils, have a richness of quality and a depth of value.

PENCILS
STICKS
AND
CRAYONS

Lithographic pencil on an acetate surface. Combined lines produce various textures.

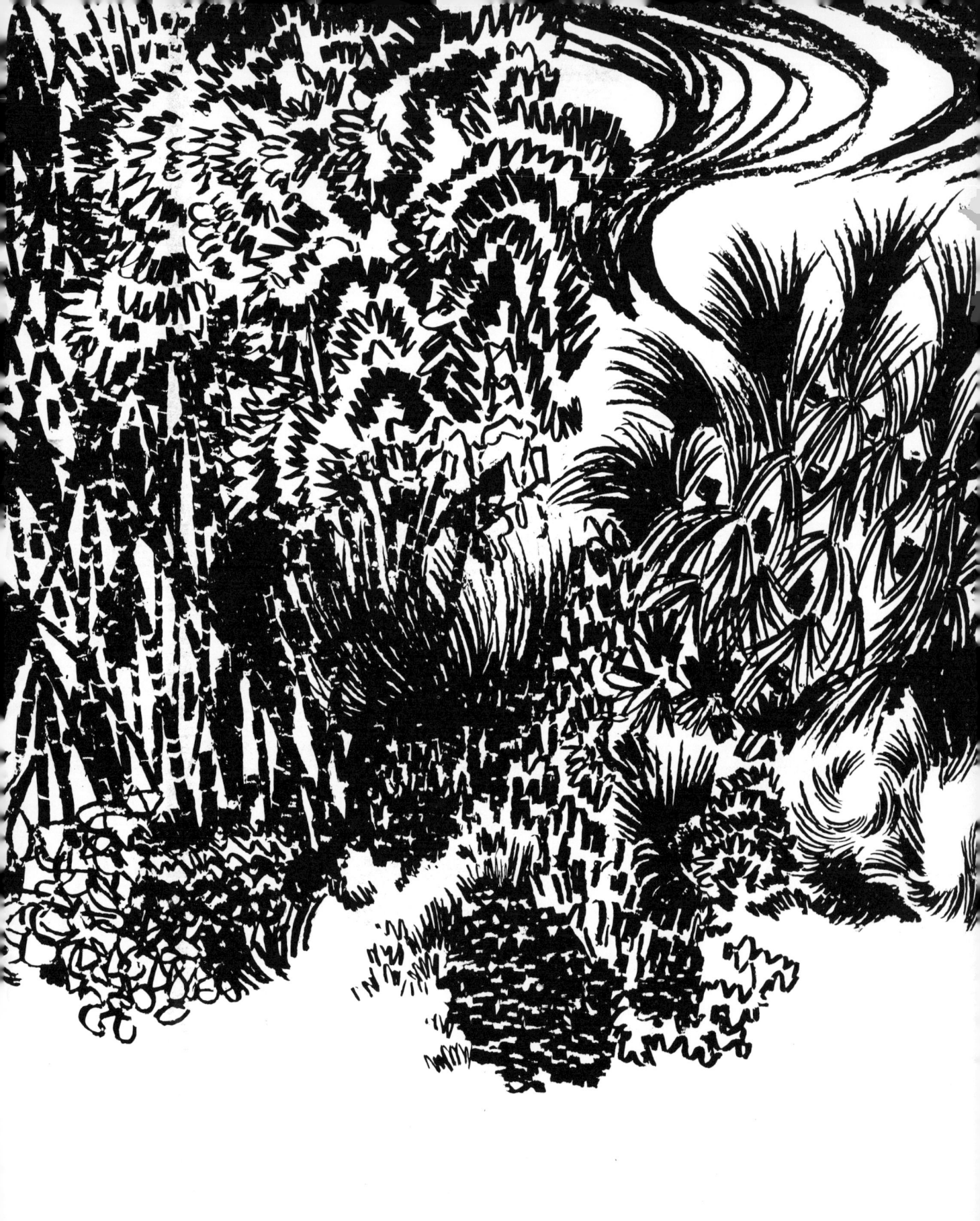

Left • Drawing done on Ross board with Korn's lithographic pencil. The board has a fine pebble texture.

Right • A simple outline drawing rendered on bond pad paper with a Blaisdell china marking pencil. Here is an example of the textured line.

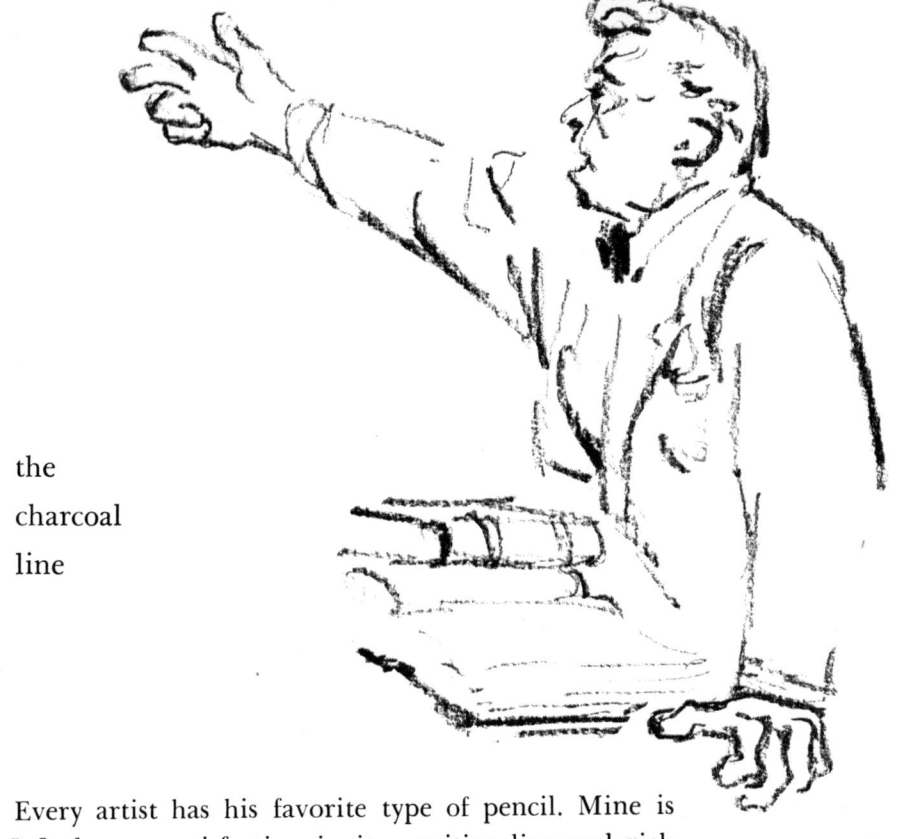

the
charcoal
line

Every artist has his favorite type of pencil. Mine is charcoal. I find great satisfaction in its sensitive line and rich quality, particularly when using it on the special charcoal papers and other highly textured surfaces.

Conté, Kohinoor, Eagle, and Blaisdell—names already familiar for other products in the art supply field—make charcoal pencils which are very good indeed. The last two named are the ones I use most frequently.

Pure charcoal sticks, not encased in wood as are the pencils, are especially pleasurable to use for the effect they produce, though their use has its hazards. The sticks, which come in varying widths and degrees of hardness, are very brittle and have a tendency to break when too much pressure is applied while drawing or sharpening the point. Even the wood-encased charcoal pencils are susceptible, for, if they are dropped, the stick may break inside the wood sheath. Careful work habits have to be cultivated for the handling of the charcoal tool.

PENCILS

STICKS

AND

CRAYONS

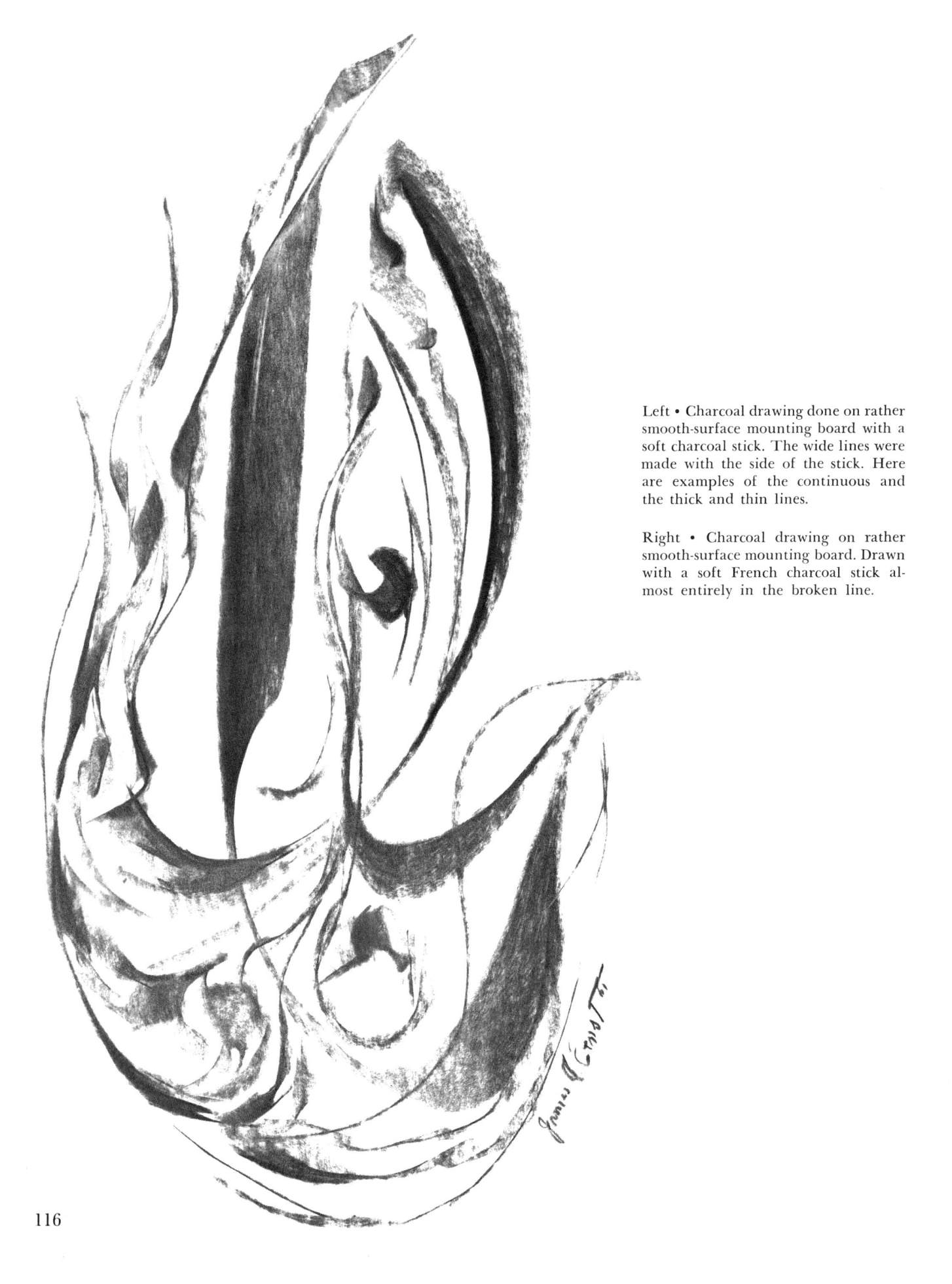

Left • Charcoal drawing done on rather smooth-surface mounting board with a soft charcoal stick. The wide lines were made with the side of the stick. Here are examples of the continuous and the thick and thin lines.

Right • Charcoal drawing on rather smooth-surface mounting board. Drawn with a soft French charcoal stick almost entirely in the broken line.

116

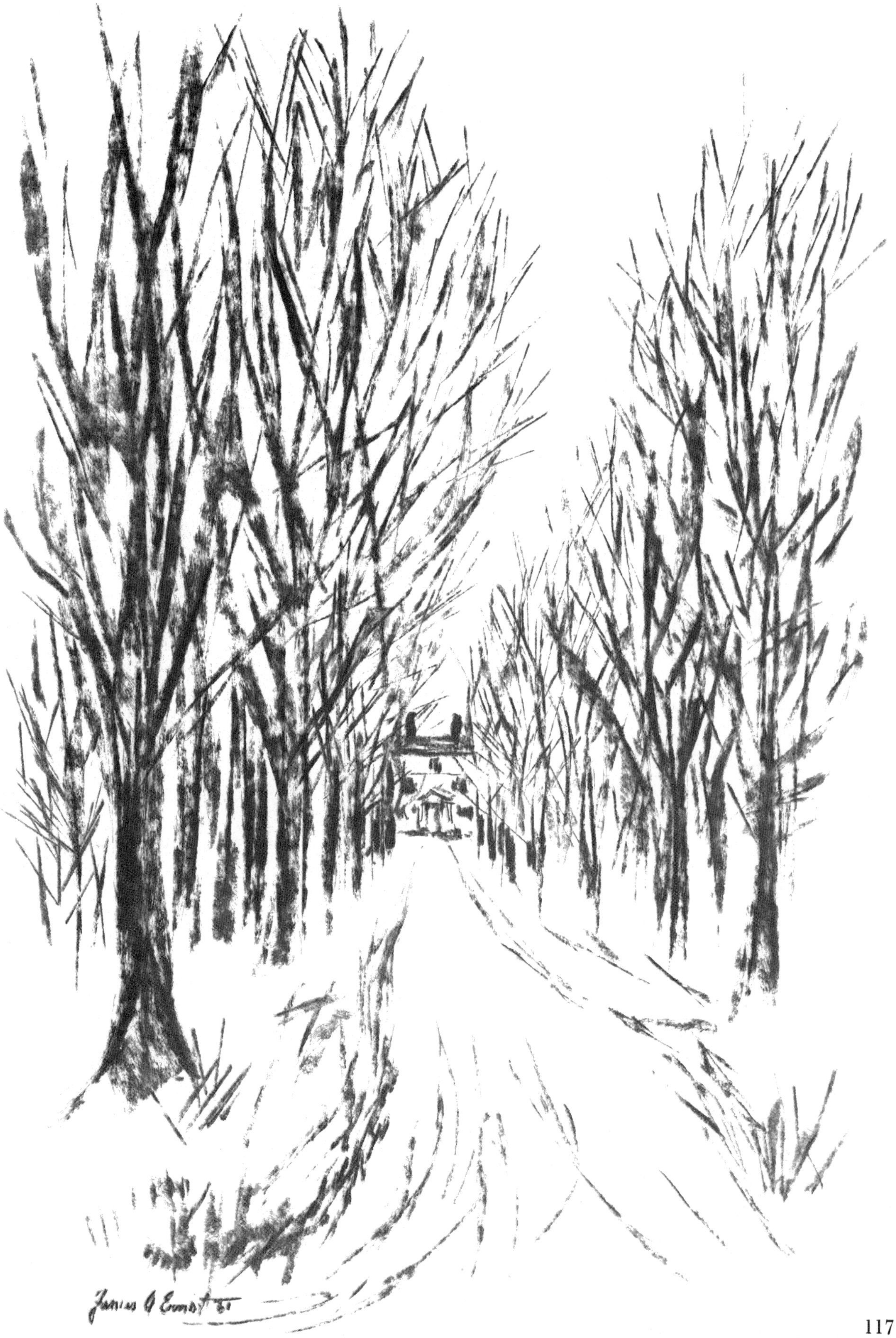

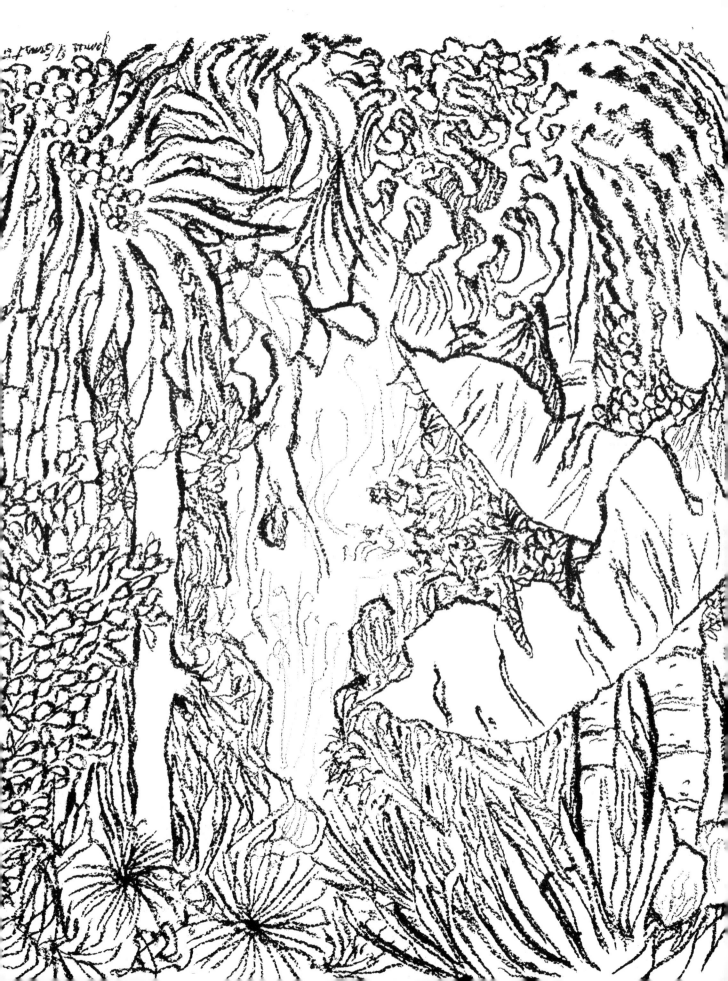

Left • Charcoal drawing
on cold pressed What-
man paper, 6B Eagle
charcoal pencil.

Right • Charcoal drawing on rather smooth-surface mounting board,
soft French charcoal stick. Movement lines around the figures are repeated around the standard. Compare the texture in this drawing with
that of the one on the left. Both pencil and charcoal stick give a rich
black with considerable variation in line width.

Charcoal line drawing on a medium surface illustration board, charcoal stick.

the

pastel

line

One might say that a pastel pencil is only as good as its point, which must be sharpened continuously. This medium comes in a single grade, quite soft. The point wears down rapidly, leading to uneven work, and breaks unexpectedly under pressure. When one learns to handle it, however, it responds better than most mediums for work with a soft graceful quality.

The special pastel papers or visualizing pad papers do very well for line work; though most papers and boards may be used, a slightly textured paper seems best.

Pastel drawings must be protected with fixative before they can be handled. The work should be cleaned with a kneaded eraser, then sprayed with great care to avoid scattering or spreading the soft particles of the pastel chalk.

PENCILS

STICKS

AND

CRAYONS

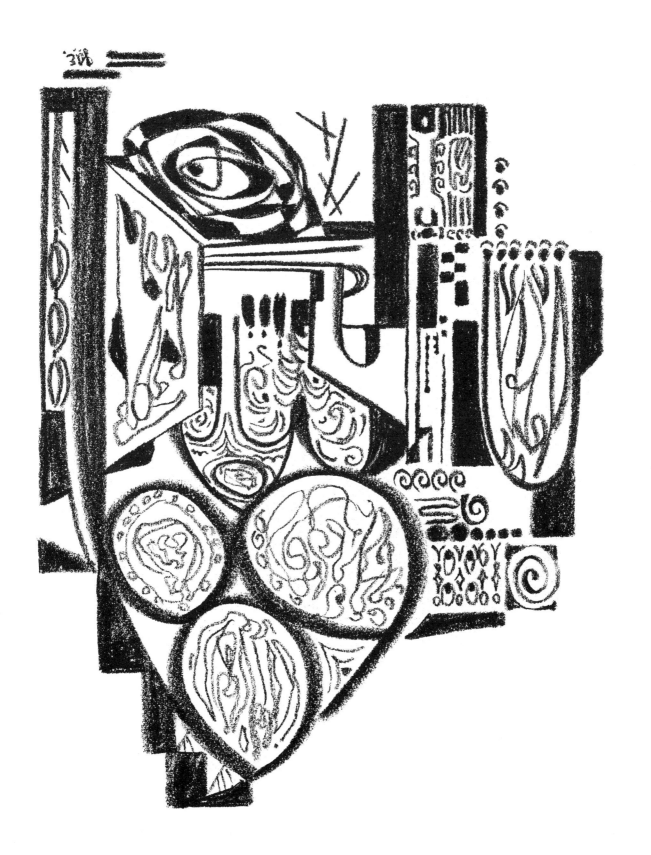

Left • Pastel line drawing on layout pad paper. Broken and continuous lines in combination with solid areas.

Right • Pastel line drawing on 3-ply kid finish Strathmore paper.

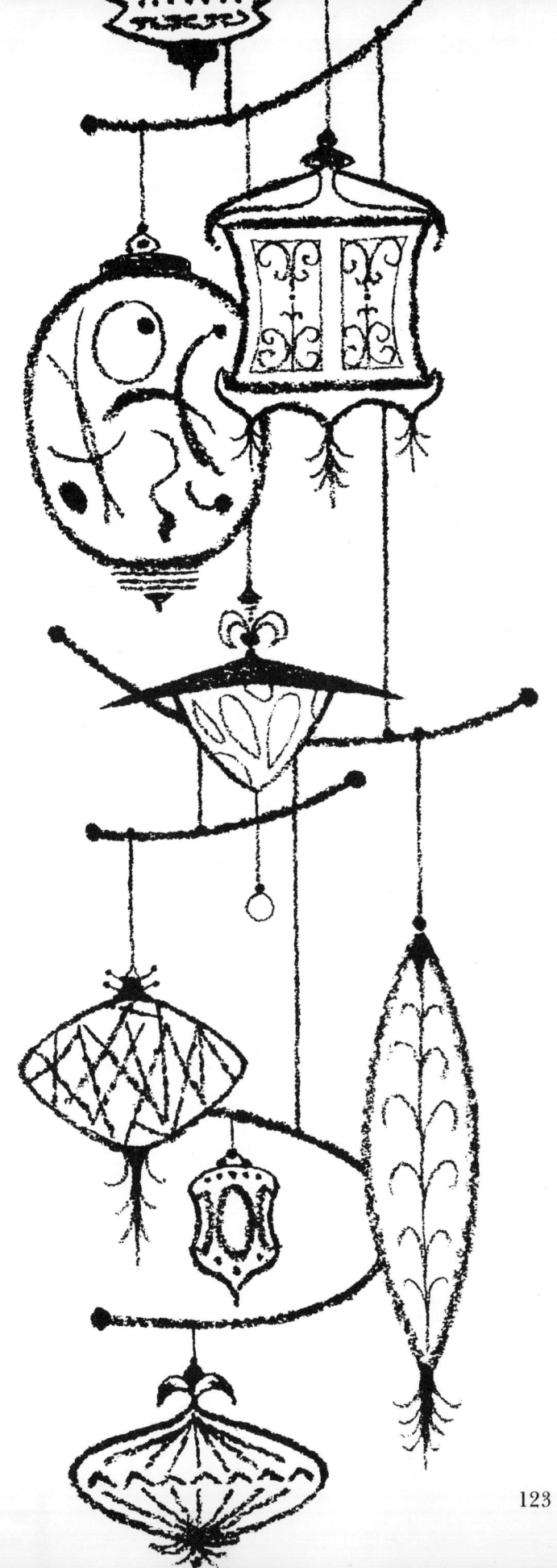

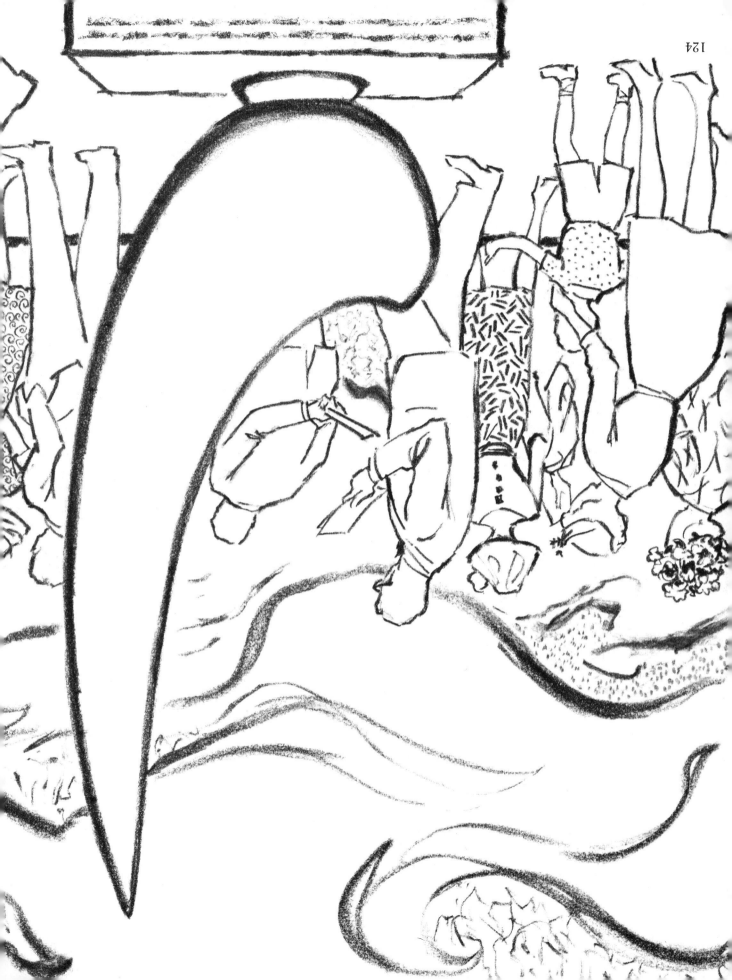

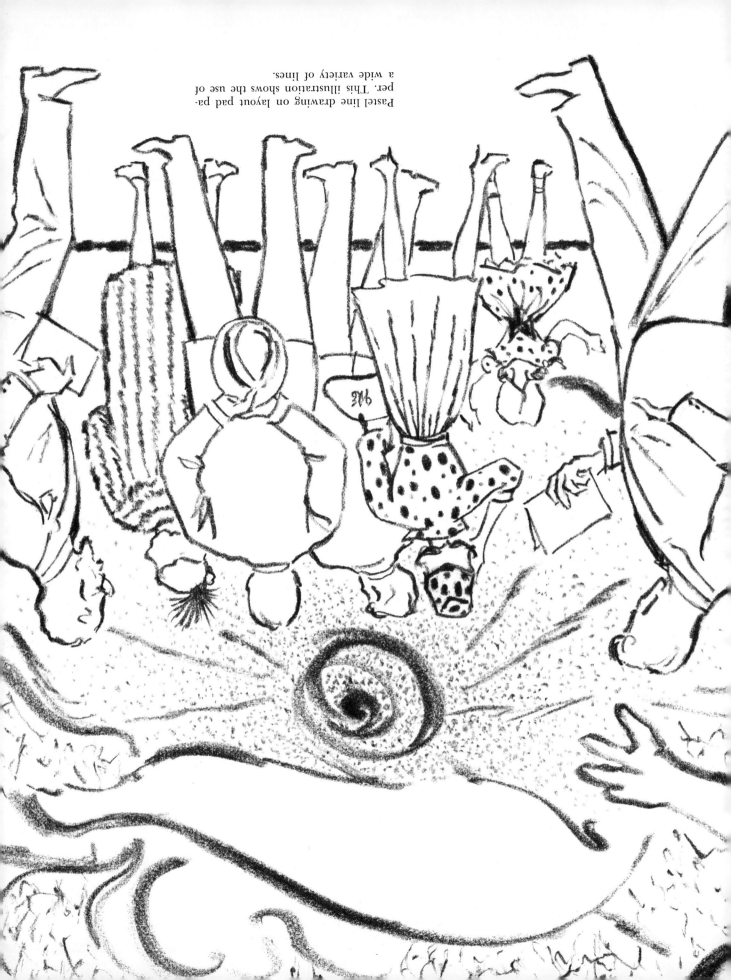
Pastel line drawing on layout pad paper. This illustration shows the use of a wide variety of lines.

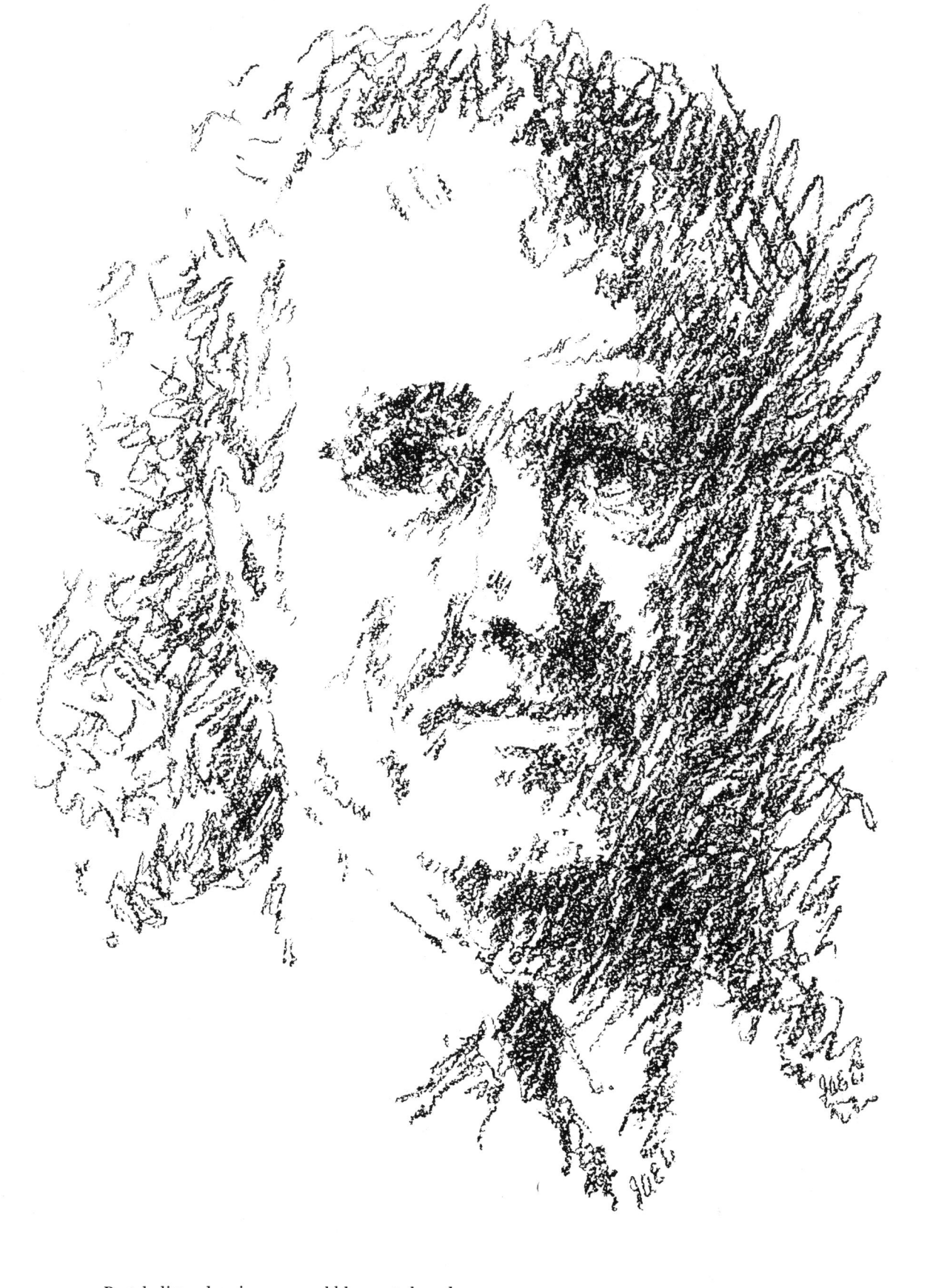

Pastel line drawing on pebble mat board.

SCRATCHBOARD

The unique distinction of the scratchboard technique is that here the artist
subtracts from rather than adds to the
working surface. As a further distinction,
it might be said that in no other medium
can so brilliant a feeling of contrast be
achieved quite so readily.

The artist, working with a sharp instrument on a prepared black scratchboard, cuts, scrapes, or scratches away the

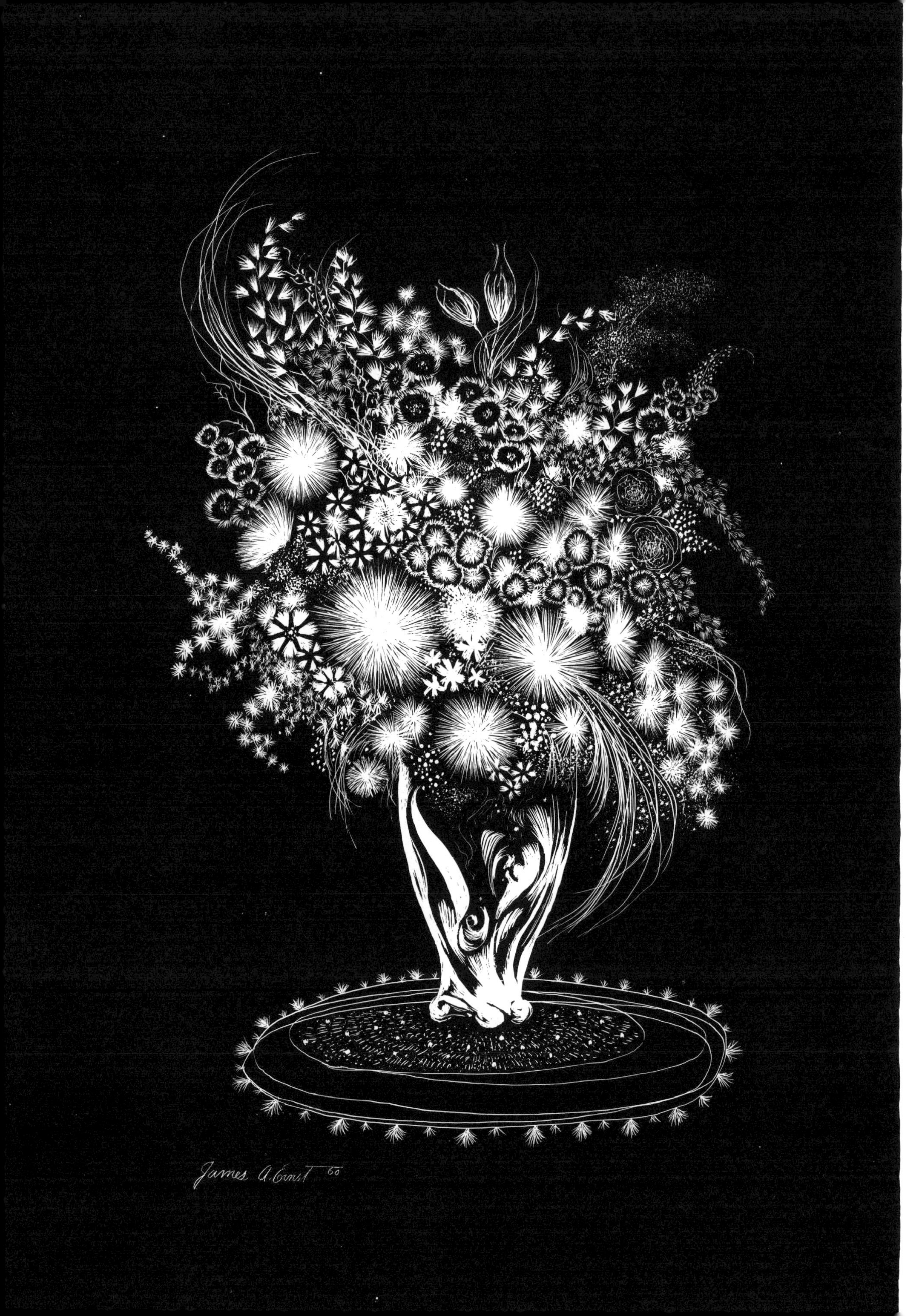

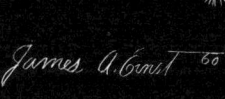

James A. Ernst '60

Left • Scratchboard drawing showing the use of combined lines scratched with a razor from a black Artone paint surface. A Gillott 290 pen was used for the black lines, done with India ink, on the unblackened area behind the flowers. The black of the flowers was drawn with a brush and Rich Art paint.

Right • Scratchboard drawing using combined lines. Some were scratched with a razor from a surface blackened with Rich Art paint and others were drawn in black ink with Gillott pen 290.

Scratchboard drawing on a slightly textured mounting board. Black paint was applied first with a brush. An occasional dry brush effect was achieved by dragging a fairly dry brush over the surface. The white lines were scratched with a razor and a surgeon's scalpel and the black pen and ink lines were made with Gillott pens 290 and 170.

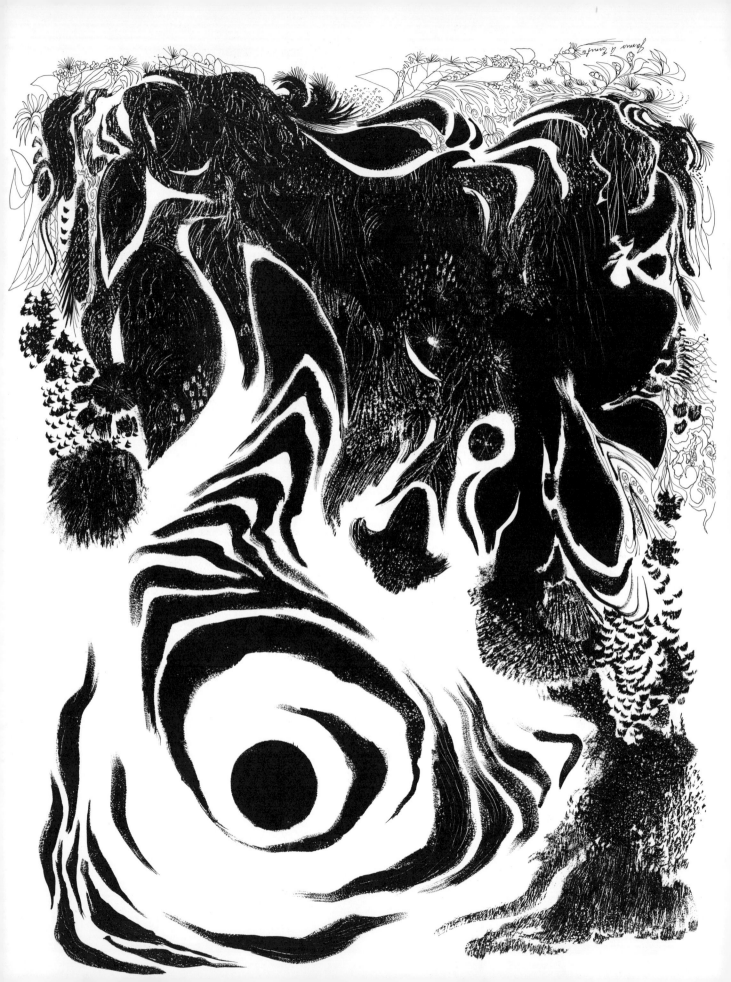

Above • Combined lines and scratchboard technique on canvas paper. Ink was applied first with a brush. Pen lines were added with a Gillott No. 290 and white lines were scratched with a surgeon's scalpel.

Right • Scratchboard drawing done on medium surface illustration board. Paint was applied first using both dry brush and split brush lines. White lines were scratched with a razor blade and pen strokes were added with Gillott pen No. 170.

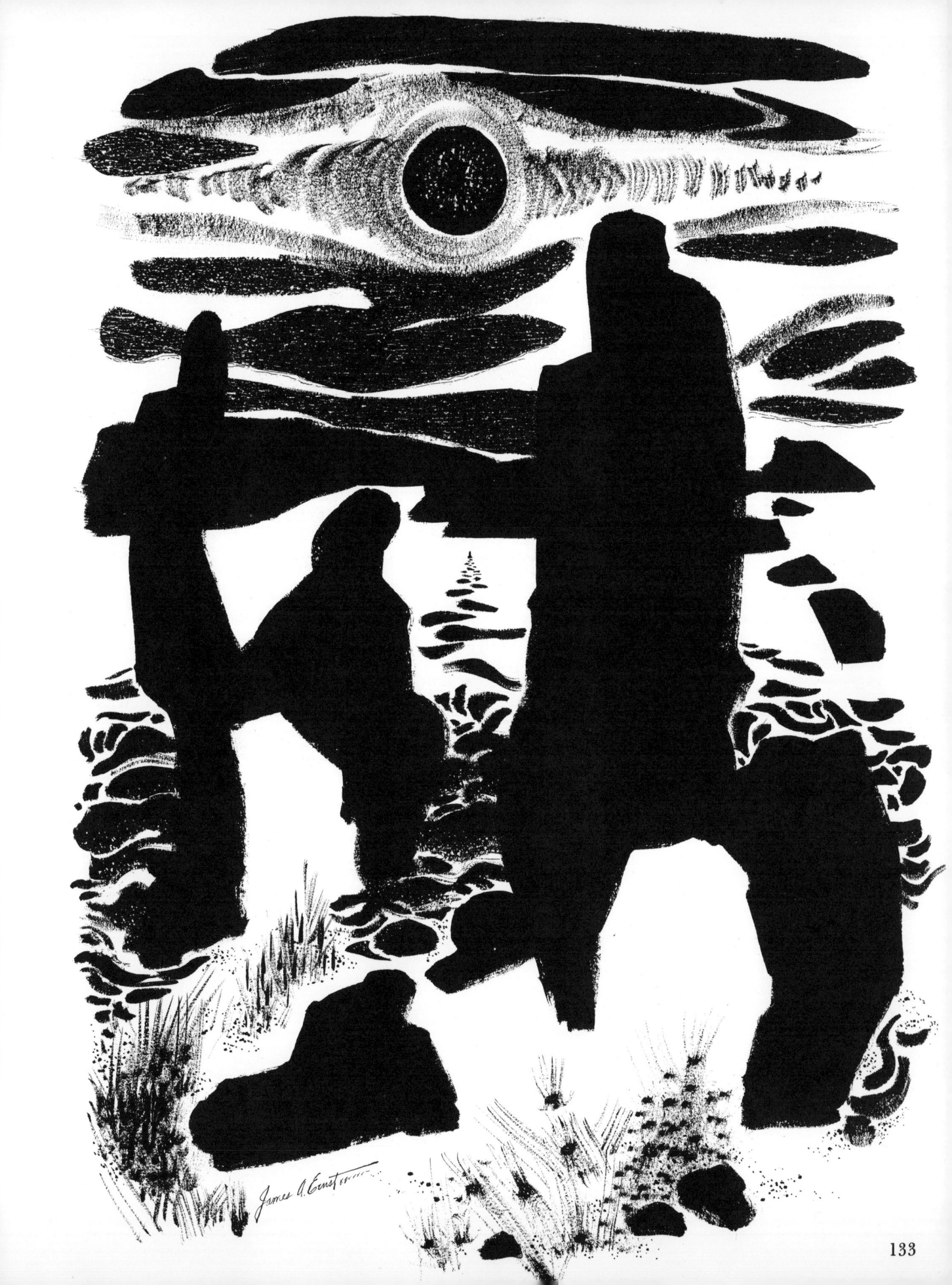

black coating, and develops his design through thus exposing the white under-surface. Almost any type of line can be achieved in this reverse process of white on black. Even the various brush lines can be simulated with multilinear tools, the many prongs of which can scratch a collection of white lines, just as the hairs of the brush lay down a collection of black lines.

Such formal equipment is not essential to scratchboard work, however. Indeed, there is wide latitude for originality in trying unconventional tools for unusual results. There are lithographic points, scratch knives, and the like to be purchased, but more or less readily available are the penknife, razor blades, a scalpel, an ordinary sewing needle, a carpet needle, nails, a small wire brush, even certain types of screws—the list can go on.

Art stores carry the black scratchboard, ready for use. They also carry the white coated board, which I prefer and which I cover with black ink or paint. The chief advantage of this method is the freedom it allows in covering the whole or only part of the board at will. I have been pleased with the effect produced by scratching white through the black in certain areas of a piece and adding black lines to the areas that were left white.

Ross and Artone make some scratchboards; Repro and Coquille boards by Grumbacher have various prepared special surfaces with textures.

Here is a technique which, perhaps more than any other, invites experiment and almost any experiment brings a result of some merit.

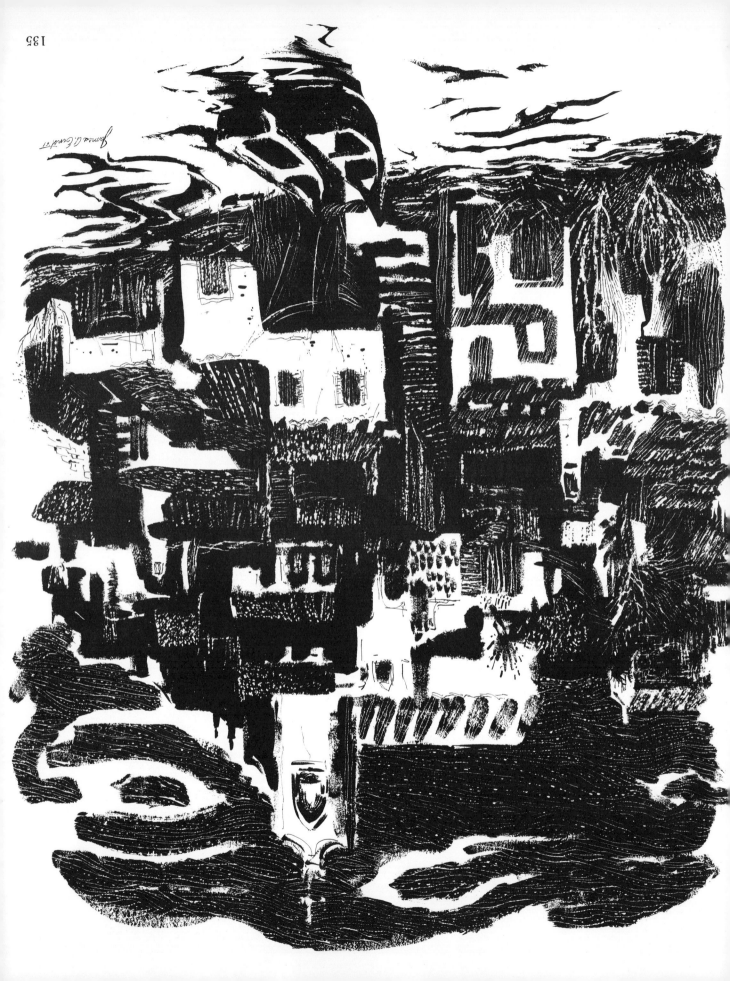

To the people of Albany

This month marks our tenth anniversary as an Albany industry. A happier ten years for us would be hard to conceive. Albany has been good to us.

You have received us warmly. You have staffed our plant with nearly three hundred of your own fine people. Each of them has helped to enhance our corporate reputation, not only in this city and state, but in the entire East. Each of them has played an important part in maintaining the excellence of our product.

You have welcomed our product enthusiastically. We are especially prideful of that.

Albany as a city, and her citizens as individuals, have made our first ten years satisfying and prosperous ones. It is our pledge, in turn, to continue to bring satisfaction to Albany, and to continue to help in creating prosperity for her citizens.

THE F. & M. SCHAEFER BREWING CO., NEW YORK and ALBANY

THE LINE IN COMMERCIAL ART

It would be my guess that, to most people outside the field, "commercial art" automatically signifies "advertising." I would guess further that "advertising" usually calls to mind a shiny page in full color.

The tremendous business of advertising probably is responsible for the majority of commercial art, but there is still a sizable minority absorbed in other areas. Similarly, a great deal of advertising is presented in the large four-color spread, but—again, guessing, for I have no interest in researching the statistics—even more ads are the smaller black-and-whites, and the bulk of these, if they use art at all, use line, with or without benday or wash.

Pick up a handful of any magazines and leaf through them to test this estimate. It is even more surely true of newspapers.

Line drawing may be the prima donna, in commercial art, or it may be the accompanist, the solo instrument or the orchestra. It often supplements a more elaborately presented major theme with background drawings which strengthen atmosphere, or establish location, or expand upon advantages of a product. It can equally well present the whole statement. It is sharp; it is clear; it transmits an idea quickly.

Among its many merits for commercial use is its steadfastness in reproduction. It does not wash out or lose tone or suffer from faulty color reproduction. Yet, it can be printed in color as well as in black and white. It will "take" on the cheapest newsprint, yet responds with dignity to the fine papers of luxury magazines. Since it is relatively inexpensive to reproduce and adapts equally well to letter press or offset methods, it is understandable that

line work is widely used and that skilled line men find ready application for their ability.

Commercial art in general—and line work in particular—is not limited to the mass media advertising of magazines and newspapers. From the giant outdoor posters along the highway, to the billboards on railroad platforms, the car cards in trains and subways, and the strips in taxis, line drawings make their direct, simple statement, usually rendered in bold treatment.

They are very much in evidence in mailers and promotion pieces, booklets, brochures, leaflets, etc. In editorial art, illustra-

two-sheet poster

Courtesy of the New York Racing Association
Agency • Batten, Barton, Durstine & Osborn, Inc.
Art Director • Tony Mandarino
Artist • Bob Peak

poster, car card

Courtesy of the Camp Fire Girls, Inc.,
and the Advertising Council, Inc.
Artist • James A. Ernst

Brush line drawing on medium surface illustration board rendered with designers gouache paints.

THE

LINE

IN

COMMERCIAL

ART

The New York Public Library
Fifth Avenue & 42nd Street
New York 18, N. Y.

postage meter slug

the corporate image

Courtesy of The New York Public Library
Lion's head • Brush and Gillott pen 290
Artist • James A. Ernst

posters

pamphlets

THE
NEW
YORK
PUBLIC
LIBRARY

EVENTS
FOR
NATIONAL
LIBRARY
WEEK

APRIL 12-18, 1959

LIBRARY
HALF-DAY
HOLIDAY

CLOSED until 2:30 p.m.
TUESDAY, MAY 23

in order that the Library Staff
may attend the celebration of
"FIFTY YEARS AT
        FIFTH and 42nd"
the fiftieth anniversary of the Central Library

THE NEW YORK PUBLIC LIBRARY

140

FILM LIBRARY
THE NEW YORK PUBLIC LIBRARY

20 West 53rd Street

film can labels

ok bags

mats

THE
NEW YORK PUBLIC LIBRARY
USE IT
ENJOY IT
SUPPORT IT

THE
NEW YORK
PUBLIC LIBRARY

ownership
book stamp

THE NEW YORK PUBLIC LIBRARY
· ASTOR LENOX & TILDEN
FOUNDATIONS

141

Courtesy of the F. & M. Schaefer Brewing Co.
New York and Albany, N. Y.
Agency • Batten, Barton, Durstine & Osborn, Inc.
Art Director • George Sanders
Artist • James A. Ernst

THE F. & M. SCHAEFER BREWING CO., NEW YORK AND ALBANY, N.Y.

THEY SAY
THEY WON'T
...BUT THEY DO!

THE
CHALLENGE
OF THE
SIXTIES

Courtesy of Batten, Barton, Durstine & Osborn, Inc.
Art Director • Hugh Miller
Artist • James A. Ernst

Spot illustration
from booklet
"Hints for people
who hate money."
Drawn with Gillott
pen No. 290.

Courtesy of Batten, Barton, Durstine & Osborn, Inc.
Art Director • Harold W. Olsen
Artist • James A. Ernst

Courtesy of the First National City Bank of New York
Agency • Batten, Barton, Durstine & Osborn, Inc.
Art Director • Harry Payne
Artist • James A. Ernst

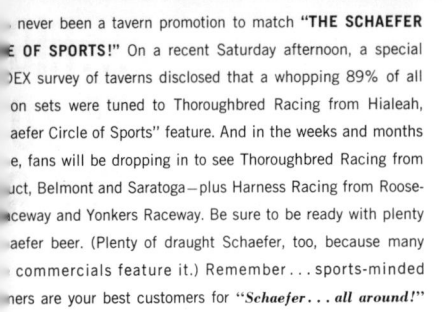

tions aid in conveying visually the written message—and the use of line holds down the cost.

Many trademarks are developed in line, as are the symbols which evoke a "corporate image." Line may be chosen here for many reasons, but a major one among them is sure to be its flexibility. Its absence of tone, makes line readily adaptable to being painted on the rigid side of a truck or being made into a resilient rubber stamp, printed on the Kraft paper of a shopping bag or engraved cleanly on the president's letterhead.

One could go on pointing out commercial use of line, for there are many more areas to be covered, even beyond greeting cards, wall paper, fabric designs, cartoons, industrial packaging.

Excellent examples of book illustration come readily to mind in fiction, in scientific and technical works among others, and in

mailers and pamphlets

THE

LINE

IN

COMMERCIAL

ART

Single-page advertisement. Illustration drawn with Gillott pens 290 and 170 with thick and thin, textured, and broken lines.

Courtesy of Batten, Barton, Durstine & Osborn, Inc.
Art Director • Harry Payne
Artist • James A. Ernst

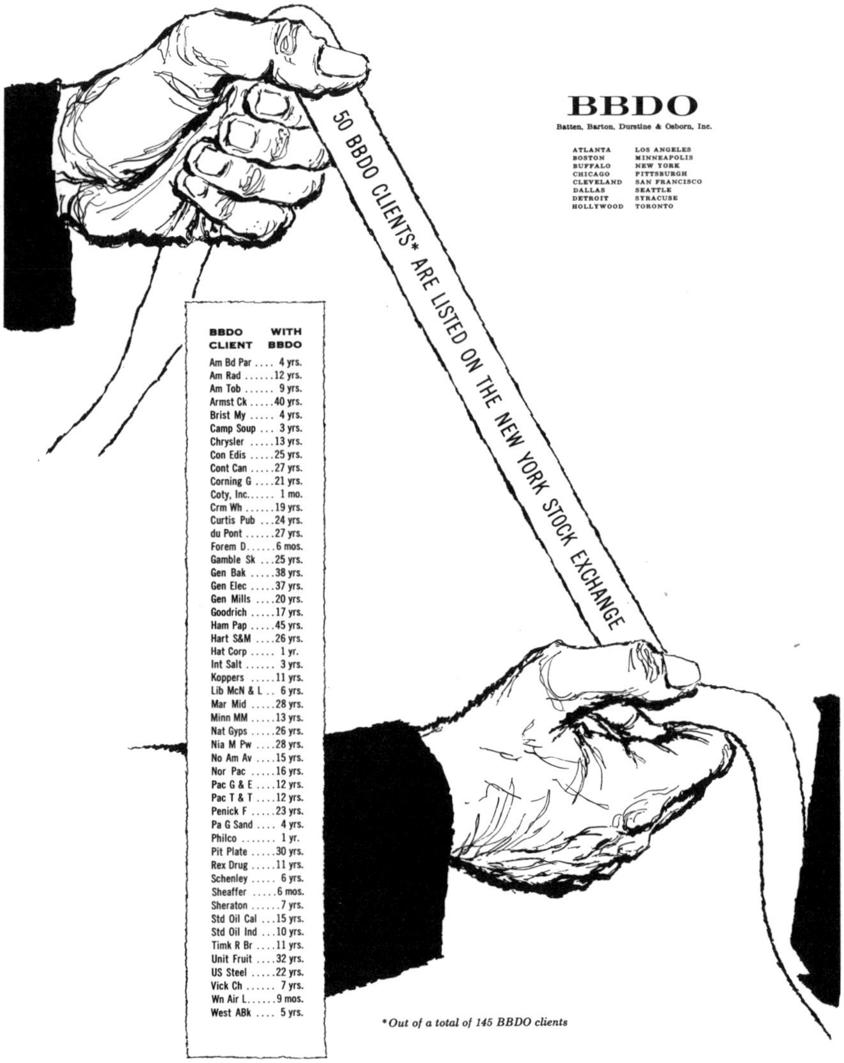

50 BBDO CLIENTS* ARE LISTED ON THE NEW YORK STOCK EXCHANGE

BBDO
Batten, Barton, Durstine & Osborn, Inc.

ATLANTA	LOS ANGELES
BOSTON	MINNEAPOLIS
BUFFALO	NEW YORK
CHICAGO	PITTSBURGH
CLEVELAND	SAN FRANCISCO
DALLAS	SEATTLE
DETROIT	SYRACUSE
HOLLYWOOD	TORONTO

BBDO CLIENT	WITH BBDO
Am Bd Par	4 yrs.
Am Rad	12 yrs.
Am Tob	9 yrs.
Armst Ck	40 yrs.
Brist My	4 yrs.
Camp Soup	3 yrs.
Chrysler	13 yrs.
Con Edis	25 yrs.
Cont Can	27 yrs.
Corning G	21 yrs.
Coty, Inc.	1 mo.
Crm Wh	19 yrs.
Curtis Pub	24 yrs.
du Pont	27 yrs.
Forem D	6 mos.
Gamble Sk	25 yrs.
Gen Bak	38 yrs.
Gen Elec	37 yrs.
Gen Mills	20 yrs.
Goodrich	17 yrs.
Ham Pap	45 yrs.
Hart S&M	26 yrs.
Hat Corp	1 yr.
Int Salt	3 yrs.
Koppers	11 yrs.
Lib McN & L	6 yrs.
Mar Mid	28 yrs.
Minn MM	13 yrs.
Nat Gyps	26 yrs.
Nia M Pw	28 yrs.
No Am Av	15 yrs.
Nor Pac	16 yrs.
Pac G & E	12 yrs.
Pac T & T	12 yrs.
Penick F	23 yrs.
Pa G Sand	4 yrs.
Philco	1 yr.
Pit Plate	30 yrs.
Rex Drug	11 yrs.
Schenley	6 yrs.
Sheaffer	6 mos.
Sheraton	7 yrs.
Std Oil Cal	15 yrs.
Std Oil Ind	10 yrs.
Timk R Br	11 yrs.
Unit Fruit	32 yrs.
US Steel	22 yrs.
Vick Ch	7 yrs.
Wn Air L	9 mos.
West ABk	5 yrs.

*Out of a total of 145 BBDO clients

WH

ABC-TV has added a *live*, full-time affiliate in Boston—WHDH-TV (Channel 5) ! Now *all* Boston can see *all* ABC-TV shows, as scheduled and programmed. And ABC-TV coverage of U.S. TV homes takes another jump—right up to 94.2%*.

Already this year, ABC-TV has added live, competitive affiliates in San Antonio, Tucson, St. Louis, Miami, Norfolk, Peoria, Omaha, Ft. Wayne, Indianapolis and Youngstown. Now WHDH-TV in Boston (the nation's sixth market) raises ABC-TV's live coverage to 82.3% of all U.S. TV homes. This season's further additions—Amarillo and Chattanooga—will push that figure to a whacking 83.1%.

That's the kind of news that sets a whole town buzzing. And an avenue, too —Madison or Michigan !

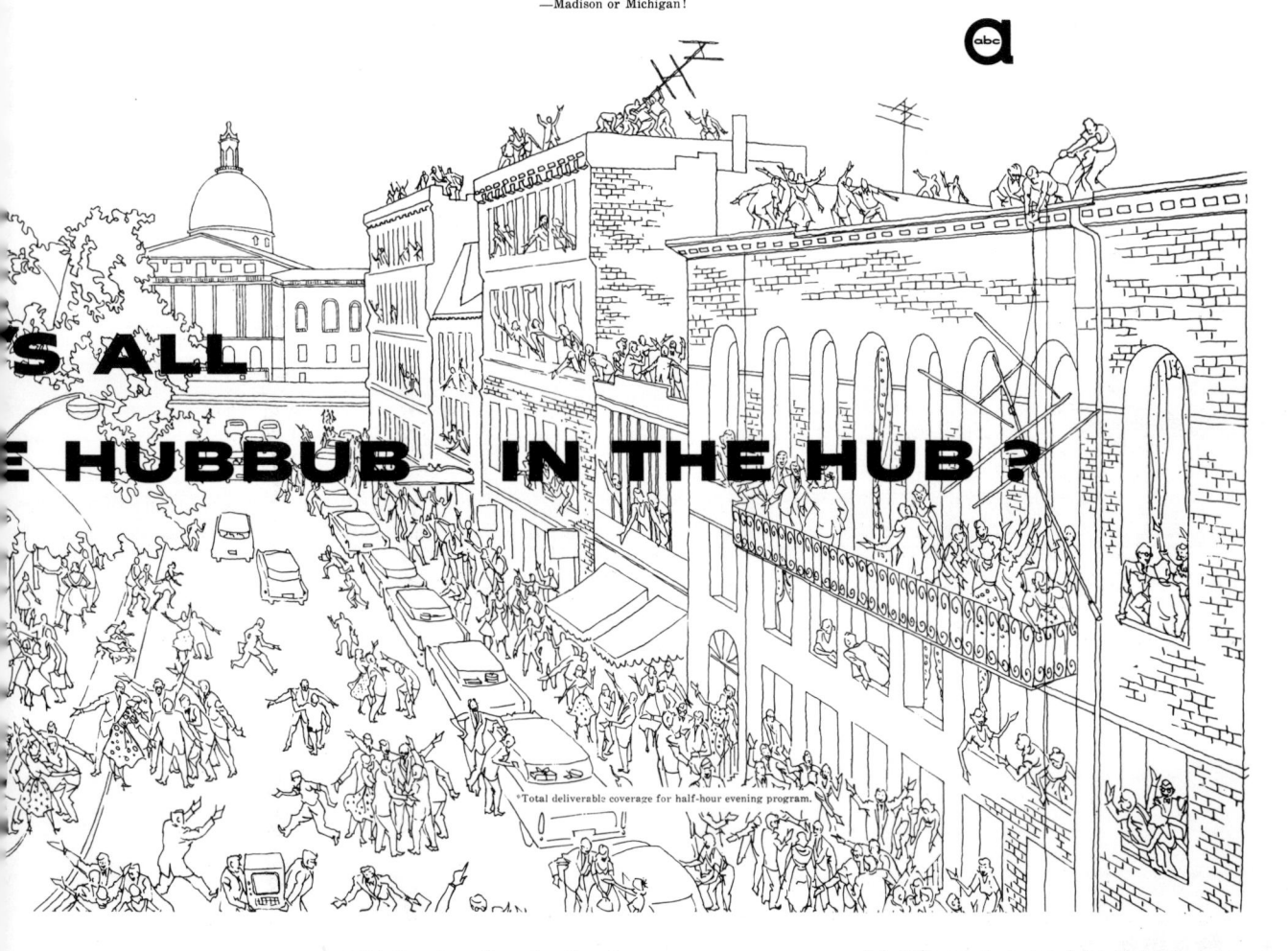

*Total deliverable coverage for half-hour evening program.

Courtesy of the American Broadcasting Co.
Agency · Batten, Barton, Durstine & Osborn, Inc.
Art Director · Victor Capellupo
Artist · James A. Ernst

Advertisement prepared for ABC television

Double-page magazine advertisement. Illustration drawn with Gillott pen No. 290 using broken and continuous lines.

145

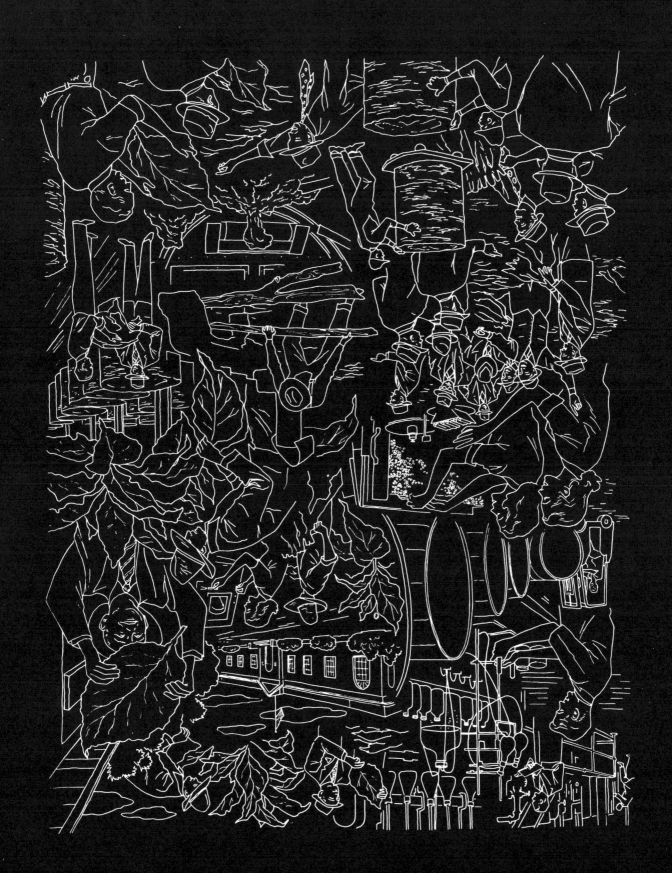

AMERICAN'S
THREE LEADING BRANDS

QUALITY PRODUCTS OF

The American Tobacco Company

AMERICA'S LEADING MANUFACTURER OF CIGARETTES

Courtesy of The American Tobacco Company
Agency · Batten, Barton, Durstine & Osborn, Inc.
Art Director · Harold W. Olsen
Artist · James A. Ernst

Above • Background drawing of the tobacco industry used as an all-over pattern with overlapping shapes to unify the entire picture field. Background and cigarette packs were held within a shape by means of a light benday. Drawn with a Gillott pen No. 170.

Left • The complete background drawing is shown in reverse with white lines on a black field.

147

Hints for
people
who <u>hate</u>
money...

Both booklet covers were drawn with Gillott pen No. 290.

Courtesy of the First National City Bank of New York
Agency • Batten, Barton, Durstine & Osborn, Inc.
Art Director • Harry Payne
Artist • James A. Ernst

... and an idea or two
for those who <u>like</u> it

the dust jackets which protect and promote them. Many more such examples are fine pieces of creative line work used to commercial advantage.

Television is multiplying the applications of line drawing in commercials, in weather maps and diagrams, and in countless other examples, presented as stills or telops, as well as on motion picture film.

Such enumeration of the uses of line is not intended to persuade the artist to clear his water colors and oils from the top of his taboret and lay them to rest inside. It is superfluous to say that most of the finest ads are in color, wash, or tone of one kind or another, not to mention the impressive advertising work which is being done with photography.

The purpose here is rather to invite alertness to the presence of line work, even in the pages which come primarily from palette or camera. Pen and ink may offer design as background to a photograph, or provide illustrative vignettes in the related text. A charcoal stroke may delineate a fold of colorful fabric or emphasize a fashion line in a gouache.

The strength of the line man's position is two-fold, depending upon his skill. If the color or tone techniques have the major attention, line can be adapted to provide detail, to add emphasis, to lend grace, or dash—or humor. If line is the only technique, then the line man has the board to himself; his past experiments and practice have put in his hand a refreshing variety of lines in which to develop his design.

THE

LINE

IN

COMMERCIAL

ART

Courtesy of California Oil Company, Eastern Division
Agency · Batten, Barton, Durstine & Osborn, Inc.
Art Director · Jack Goldsmith
Artist · Jack Goldsmith

Hy Finn character on television commercials.

Hallmark:

The proud craftsman's signature

A craftsman's hallmark is a zealously guarded possession. He puts it only on those of his works he considers particularly worthy. This hallmark is his way of saying, "I made this...and I am proud of it."

The California Oil Company's hallmark is the chevron you see above. We put it on our products, our equipment, our stations. It is worn with pride by our employees. It is displayed with pride wherever the company is represented.

The Chevron hallmark is our way of saying, "There is nothing finer." We are painstakingly careful that each product and station that bears it lives up to that promise. Our customers, through their experience with our products, have come to know it as a symbol of excellence, a guarantee of quality.

Today, at all Calso Stations, a new gasoline bears the proud Chevron hallmark: Chevron Supreme. This new, high-octane fuel is produced by some of America's most modern refineries...and sold in 26 states through more than 14,000 Dealers.

Eastern motorists will discover — as have millions from Canada to Mexico — that Chevron Supreme completely lives up to our hallmark's guarantee of quality and excellence. For in every way this is a product truly worthy of the proud Chevron hallmark.

CALSO
STATIONS

THE CALIFORNIA OIL COMPANY

Look for this CHEVRON
—your guarantee of quality products.

Courtesy of California Oil Company, Eastern Division
Agency • Batten, Barton, Durstine & Osborn, Inc.
Art Director • Jack Rindner
Artist • James A. Ernst

Five-column, 200-line newspaper advertisement drawn with Gillott pen 290 using the broken line. Note the over-all weight.

Four-column, 200-line newspaper advertisement drawn with a Gillott 290. Note use of the broken line.

Courtesy of National Gypsum Company
Agency • Batten, Barton, Durstine & Osborn, Inc.
Art Director • Harry Payne
Artist • James A. Ernst

You, too, can have a cool house this summer!

"Here's how I lowered room temperatures as much as 15° with Gold Bond TWINSULATION°"

Our house was a hotbox. One broiling night last summer my wife and I were sitting in the living room. The house was stifling . . . the upstairs rooms a hotbox. Then I spotted an ad in a magazine that said: "Why swelter? Have a cool house with Gold Bond Twinsulation. You can install it yourself in a jiffy."

What my lumber dealer told me. Next morning I asked our lumber dealer about Twinsulation. "Jim," he said, "I sell all kinds of insulation. But Twinsulation is so much better that I put it in my own attic. The way it's cooled our entire house is unbelievable."

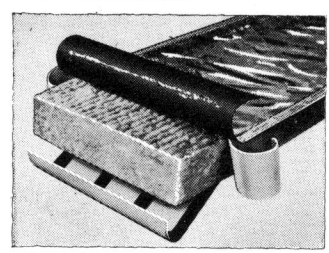

Two insulations in one. "Look here, Jim. Ordinary insulation is made of just one material. But Twinsulation is a combination of *two* insulations. See? Aluminum outside to *reflect* heat, rock wool inside to *block* it. It's double insulation. Twice as effective."

Easy to install. "Is it hard to install?" I asked. "I'm no great handy man." "It's simple," said Fred. "First of all, Twinsulation is real easy to handle. Here, lift this piece. Light, isn't it? And all you do is lay these blankets between the rafters in your attic—or staple 'em between the studs. I have the stapler for you to use, too."

Did it in one afternoon. I started stapling the Twinsulation blankets in our attic that next Saturday . . . and actually finished the whole job in less than four hours. The wife and youngster came up to watch me for a while, and darned if my boy didn't borrow the stapler from me and get going himself. Sorta fun to do, you know.

Cooler in summer, warmer in winter. Gold Bond Twinsulation is about the smartest buy we ever made. All summer our house was much, *much* cooler. On the hottest nights we *slept*. And last winter, not only was the house warmer, but our fuel bills were lower.

See your Gold Bond® TWINSULATION dealer today!

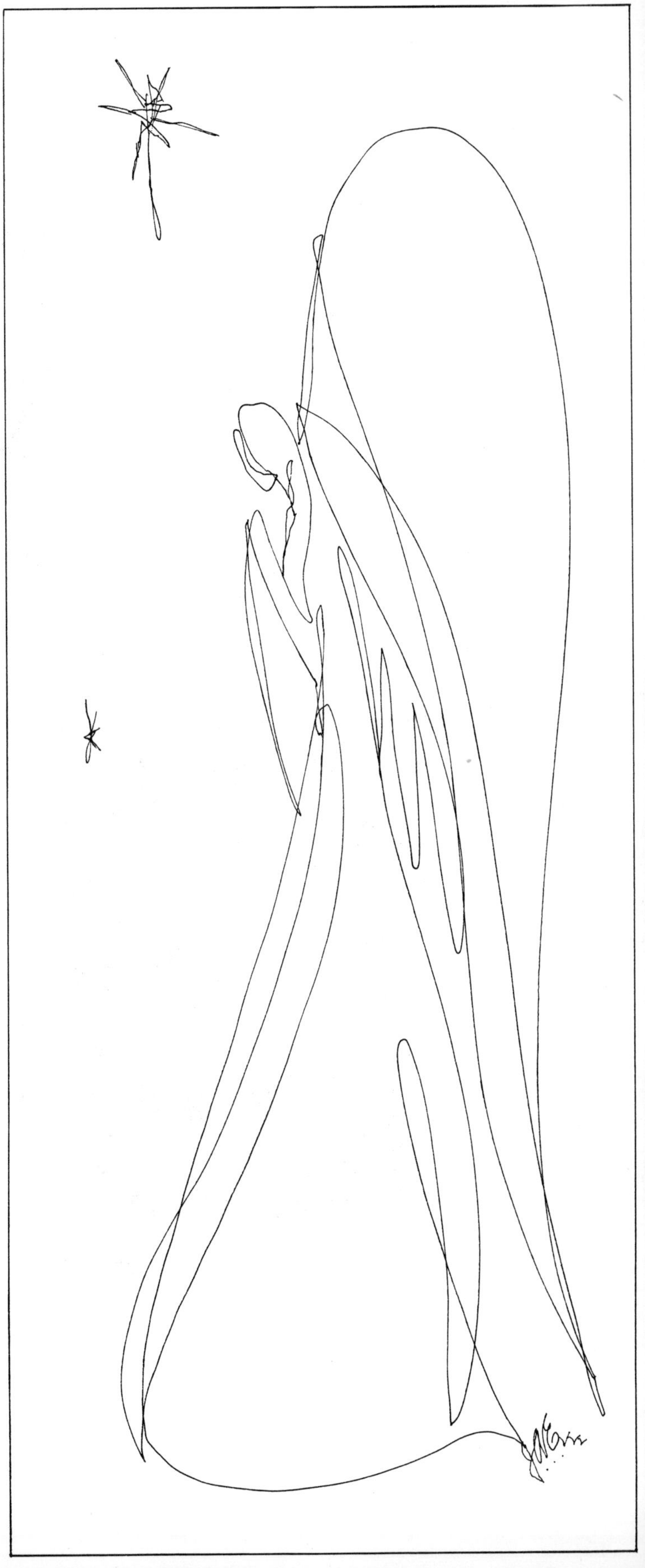

Greeting cards
Left • Textured and broken lines.
Right • The continuous line.
Both drawn with Gillott pen 290.

End of the line • Drawn with pen and
brush on canvas paper, Gillott pen 290.

154

END OF THE LINE

There is, of course, no end to a line, mathematically, since the line continues on in space. There is an end, however, to what anyone can contribute profitably in the way of information about drawing the line. From that point on, practice must take over if progress is to be made in the satisfying execution of line drawing.

For the most part, one must make one's own mistakes and gain from his own experiences. Yet, occasionally, a fellow artist's narration of some incident may seem apt enough to be remembered and to be useful.

One experience which came my way in early free-lance days taught me a rule which I still follow when occasion arises. In preparing my portfolio of illustrations to show to art directors, I began by trying to cover all possibilities and show everything I could do. I didn't object to lugging a heavy case: I guess it didn't occur to me that anyone else might object to looking at its entire contents.

Luckily for me, before long I met one man whose kindness I won't forget. He seemed interested in my work and took considerable time to talk with me. He looked at all my pieces all right —looked at them and weeded out the bulk of what I had!

"Art directors are as human as anybody," he said. "They get tired of looking at drawing after drawing, no matter how good the work is. It doesn't take many pieces for them to estimate the quality of your ability and your probable range. Keep ten as your absolute maximum. Never show more than ten pieces."

It was that same man who also suggested that I include two or three fine arts pieces among the ten. "The art director will be glad to have a change," he said, "and besides, they will tell him a good deal more about you than your draftsmanship."

As for the fine arts pieces, they proved a good way to get a start—selling them to magazines as spot illustrations, and to the

smaller local publications first, before aiming at the deluxe periodicals.

I have had my share of experiences with the "freeze," a state experienced by artists when they are faced with a white sheet of paper, when no approach seems right, no idea will come. I have survived it by substituting a large scratch pad for the sheet and wrestling with that until something loosened up enough to get me into a beginning.

Whether an artist is working "outside" or "inside"—free lance or in an agency—he is drawing for somebody; say, for a client with assignment from an art director. In the first place, I suppose all of us feel that there is never enough time allowed. Within an agency, even though work on an ad may begin weeks ahead, there are inevitable delays whether for decisions, for new ideas to be worked out, for material to come back from the client, for many reasons. Suddenly the deadline looms and the art work is yet to be done—overnight, or in an hour and a half! Deadlines are immovable, and the artist has no choice but to get the work done. Perhaps he should have had a day and a half, to be able to meet his own best standard; but he hasn't So, he does it in an hour and a half. Sometimes—not always—this is the way with commercial art, but then every job has its hazards.

Whether hurried or not, I keep two small tools at hand which enable me to test my work as I go along. They are a reducing glass and an enlarging glass. Comprehensives to be shown to a client must be done in the actual size planned for final use, but the finished work may be in any size so long as it will scale properly to final space requirements.

If I am working large, I peer through my reducing glass to check whether my design, which looks so good with lots of air around, is going to seem crowded and busy when brought down

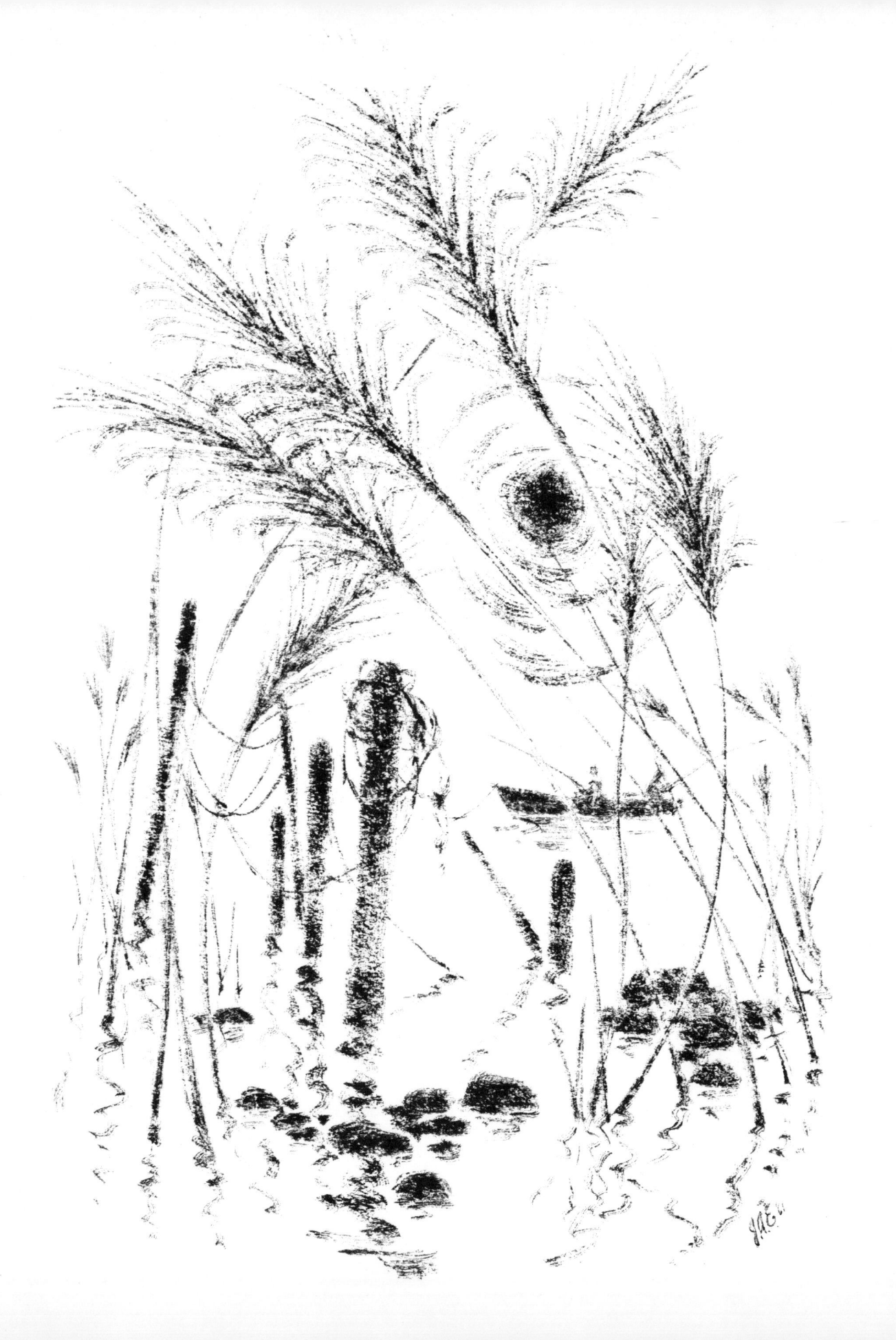

in size; whether my lines or solids are going to be so close together that they may "go to mud" in reproduction.

I use the enlarging glass to examine the quality of the line itself, to see how its character holds up, to see that there are no breaks or too thin places. One never knows, despite original purpose, to what use art work may later be put, and if it should be blown up to poster size, for instance, I want to be sure that my line can pass the test.

There is nothing in the world an artist can do to guard against the client's changing his mind, or the art director's revising the approach, or the copywriter's shifting the emphasis, *after* the artist has begun working. The one thing he *can* do to protect against fruitless effort is to be as sure as it possible to be that he understands the instructions given him, and understands them thoroughly. Words can be tricky; they can start a piece of work

END
OF
THE
LINE

off in a direction quite different from the intent of the assignment, and a whole job can go wrong as a result. It is a good idea to repeat your instructions when they are given, and to do a sketch to illustrate and test your understanding of them, before you leave the person who gives the assignment.

Once you understand, don't stray afield unless you are sure you have that leeway. Even if you are encouraged to take some freedom, it may be well to check back to be sure you aren't taking too much. The art director may have chosen you because he thinks he knows your style and he may not relish a surprise.

On the other hand, there are those rare occasions, those spirit-lifting opportunities, when you *are* chosen because your versatility and your imagination and ingenuity are known, and you are given carte blanche in interpreting the specific idea assigned you. Then is when you most enjoy using that skill which you have acquired for variety and flexibility of expression; then is when all the experiment and practice bring their satisfying reward.

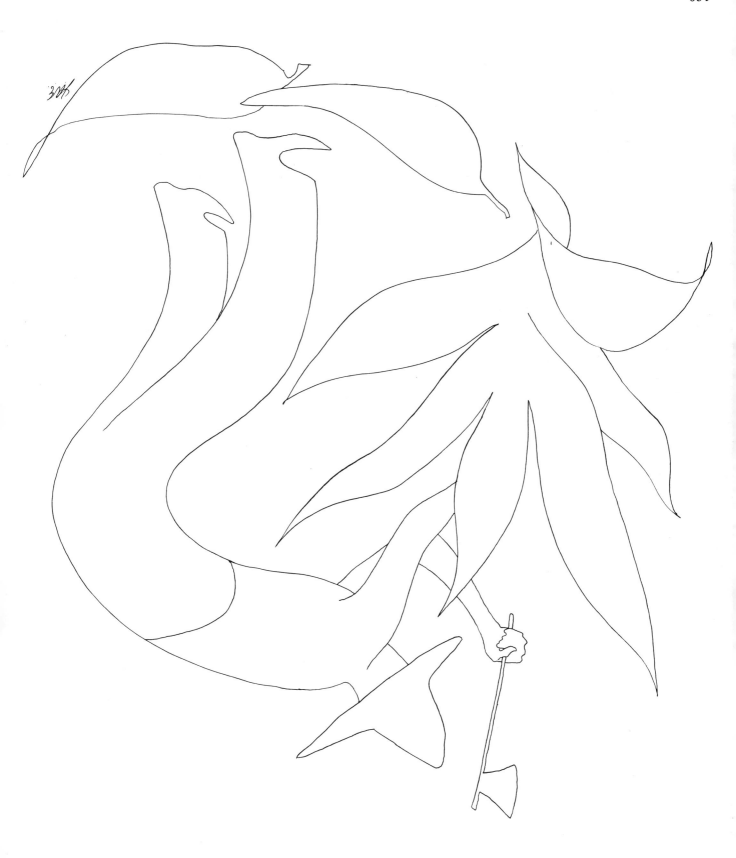

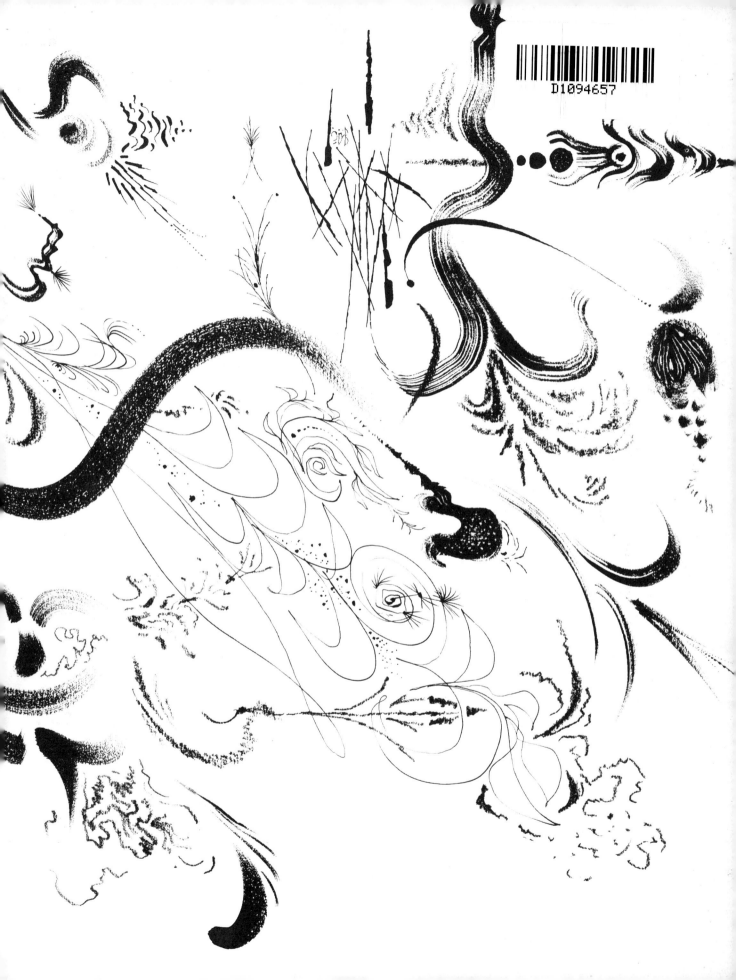